# Lessons from NAFTA:
# The High Cost of "Free Trade"

Editors:
Karen Hansen-Kuhn and Steve Hellinger

Authors:
Sarah Anderson, Manuel Ángel Gómez Cruz,
John Dillon, Ed Finn, John Foster, Karen Hansen-Kuhn,
Alberto Arroyo Picard, David Ranney,
and Rita Schwentesius Rindermann

Canadian Centre for Policy Alternatives

National Library of Canada Cataloguing in Publication

Lessons from NAFTA : the high cost of free trade / edited by Karen Hansen-Kuhn and Steve Hellinger.

Includes bibliographical references.
ISBN 0-88627-333-1

1. Canada. Treaties, etc. 1992 Oct. 7. 2. Free trade—North America. 3. North America—Economic conditions. 4. North America—Social conditions. I. Hansen-Kuhn, Karen II. Hellinger, Steve III. Canadian Centre for Policy Alternatives.

HF1746.L47 2003          382'.917          C2003-906308-9

Printed and bound in Canada

Published by

Canadian Centre for Policy Alternatives
Suite 410, 75 Albert Street
Ottawa, ON K1P 5E7
Tel 613-563-1341    Fax 613-233-1458
http://www.policyalternatives.ca
ccpa@policyalternatives.ca

# Contents

# Acknowledgements

This document was prepared by Mexican, U.S., and Canadian members of the Hemispheric Social Alliance's Monitoring and Alternatives Committee. Each chapter reflects the perspectives of its respective author or authors.

We would like to thank the John D. and Catherine T. MacArthur Foundation, the Rockefeller Foundation, and the Solidago Foundation, whose generous support made the writing of this study possible.

We also wish to thank Ed Finn, Kerri-Anne Finn and Bruce Campbell of the Canadian Centre for Policy Alternatives for their assistance with the editing and publication of the English version of this study.

We are particularly grateful to Karen Hansen-Khun and Steve Hellinger for serving as overall editors of this document and co-ordinators of the Hemispheric Social Alliance's Monitoring and Analysis Committee.

For more information on the Hemispheric Social Alliance and the Spanish version of this study please visit our web site at www.asc-hsa.org

# Summary
## by Ed Finn

The corporate and political advocates of the North American Free Trade Agreement (NAFTA) continue to defend this trade deal and even to claim that its effects on the workers and consumers of all three countries—Canada, the United States, and Mexico—have been enormously beneficial.

In fact, the impact of NAFTA on most of the people in all three countries has been devastating. The agreement has destroyed more jobs than it has created, depressed wages, worsened poverty and inequality, eroded social programs, undermined democracy, enfeebled governments, and greatly increased the rights and power of corporations, investors, and property holders.

NAFTA has also been used to weaken Canada's sovereignty and promote its economic assimilation by the United States. It has led to greater pressure on Canada and Mexico to conform to U.S. foreign policy objectives. Most alarmingly, the three governments are bent on extending this failed model to other countries in Central and South America and the Caribbean in the proposed Free Trade Area of the Americas (FTAA). Before leaping into that abyss, citizens and policy-makers throughout the hemisphere should stop and look at the concrete results of this trilateral trade agreement.

On NAFTA's 10th anniversary, researchers based in all three countries have assessed the agreement's consequences and found them to be overwhelmingly negative. Their findings are presented in the following summary of their longer studies.

## Canada

The era of Canada-U.S. free trade began with the signing of the Canada-US Free Trade Agreement (CUFTA) in 1988, and it triggered a phenomenal growth in commerce between the two countries—from a value of US$116 billion in 1985 to more than US$240 billion by 2002. Between 1989 and 2002, Canadian exports to the U.S. rose by 221%, while imports from the U.S. went up by 162%.

Politicians and media pundits point to these figures as "proof" of NAFTA's "success," but such crude mercantilist measures fail to conform to the actual economic rationale for free trade. One of the arguments, for example, was that free trade would increase Canada's disappointing rate of economic growth, which in the eight years prior to CUFTA had averaged only 1.9% per capita per year. Instead, in the first five years of free trade, real GDP growth per capita was actually negative, averaging -0.4% a year. The GDP rate rose after NAFTA came into effect, but for the entire free trade era has averaged 1.6% annually, which is still below the pre-CUFTA rate.

**Productivity:** The main economic rationale for free trade, however, was that increases in two-way trade would boost Canadian productivity, and thus lead to higher wages and rising living standards. What actually happened was that, between 1989 and 1993, average labour productivity in the business sector grew at an annual rate of 0.6%, which was less than half of its rate of growth over the previous eight years (1981-88), when productivity rose by 1.6% per year. Over the same CUFTA period (1989-93), real (inflation-adjusted) hourly wages in Canada rose by only 0.2% per year—less than half the 0.5% average increase over the previous pre-free-trade years.

Productivity growth regained and even exceeded its pre-CUFTA rate in the NAFTA years from 1994 to 2002, averaging 2.1%, but real wage gains continued to lag behind increases in productivity as employers, not workers, reaped the benefits of higher hourly output.

A comparison of productivity increases and labour costs in the key manufacturing sector in the U.S., Canada and Mexico from 1993 to June 2002 shows that, over this period, the cumulative increase in Canadian output per hour was only 14.52%, while the increase in the U.S. amounted to 51.98%, and in Mexico 53%. Labour costs, measured in U.S. dollars, actually fell in all three countries, further evidence that productivity gains were not passed on to workers in any of the three NAFTA countries.

In the years prior to CUFTA, manufacturing productivity in Canada stood at 83% of the U.S. level. By 2000, it had dropped to only 65%. So the productivity gap widened rather than narrowed, as promised by the proponents of free trade.

One of the reasons for the widening productivity gap is the dominance of foreign transnational corporations in Canadian manufacturing, since foreign corporations typically invest much less than domestic firms in industrial research and development.

**Investment:** The promoters of free trade predicted that it would lead to new foreign direct investment (FDI) in Canada and to the expansion of U.S.-owned branch plants. Such U.S. investment did grow by a modest C$36.8 billion in the CUFTA years, and by a further C$102 billion under NAFTA up to 2002. But most of this "investment" took the form of takeovers of Canadian firms, not new "greenfield" investments. From 1985 to 2002, there were 10,052 foreign takeovers of Canadian companies, 6,437 of them by U.S. corporations.

Of all the new direct foreign investment in Canada over this period, an extraordinary 96.6% was for takeovers and only a meagre 3.4% for new business. And to make matters even worse, many of these takeovers were financed through borrowing within Canada.

At the same time, there was a marked increase in Canadian FDI in the U.S., showing a pattern of disinvestment from Canada. By 2002, Canadians held about US$133 billion worth of FDI in the U.S., three times more than they did in 1990. But this doesn't mean that Canadian investors are taking control of key U.S. industries. As Mel Hurtig points out, "There is not one single industry in the U.S. that is majority-foreign-owned and/or foreign-controlled." As of 1999, Canadians owned less than 0.6% of U.S. industrial investment.

**Job losses and labour "flexibility":** In describing its "success," NAFTA boosters credit the agreement with increasing employment and prosperity in all three countries. Admittedly, during NAFTA's first nine years, employment in Canada grew by 19%, representing a gain of 2.7 million new jobs. But fewer than half these new jobs were full-time. And this apparently rosy period of Canadian job gains under NAFTA should be set against the prior six-year period of heavy job losses under CUFTA. Between 1988 and 1994, Canada lost 334,000 manufacturing jobs, equivalent to 17% of total manufacturing employment in the year before CUFTA came into effect. Canada's official unemployment rate rose from an average of 7.8% in 1988-90 to 11% during 1991-93.

During the first 13 years under CUFTA and NAFTA, Canada created less than half as many full-time jobs as during the previous 13 years. Moreover, many of the jobs created during the NAFTA period have been part-time, insecure jobs with fewer benefits, particularly for women. A study on labour market conditions in Canada under NAFTA found that "part-time workers—overwhelmingly women—earn just two-thirds the wages of equivalent full-time workers, and less than 20% receive benefits from their employers."

The year 2002 was marked by a superficially impressive increase of 560,000 jobs in Canada, but 40% of them were part-time and another 17% were self-employed. Thus, while the overall employment statistics look positive, the process of creating a more "flexible" workforce continues.

**Social programs:** Canada's business élite has consistently argued that, for Canada to be competitive in NAFTA, its social programs would have to be cut to match the generally inferior U.S. levels. This process started just four months after the implementation of CUFTA when the Mulroney government brought down its 1989 budget. It imposed cuts to Unemployment Insurance, old Age Security, and federal transfers to the provinces for health care and education. This pattern of social spending cuts continued throughout the mandate of the Tory government, and was accelerated by the Liberals after they took office in 1993—especially in their 1995 budget which included $29 billion in spending cuts over the next three years.

The most stark example of this downward harmonization of Canadian social policy is what happened to unemployment insurance. The UI system has been slashed repeatedly by both Tory and Liberal governments to conform to the lower standards prevailing in the U.S. Whereas in 1989, 87% of the unemployed in Canada qualified for UI benefits (as compared to 52% in the U.S.), by 2001 only 39% of jobless Canadians could qualify for coverage. These deep cuts hurt more women than men because women more frequently work part time and enter and leave the workforce more often due to child-care responsibilities.

**Trade disputes:** The Mulroney government and other free trade pushers claimed that a free trade agreement with the U.S. would exempt Canada from American anti-dumping and countervailing duty measures. This promise, too, proved false. Canada remains subject to U.S. arbitrary actions such as the punitive U.S. duty on Canadian softwood lumber exports. All that Canada got was a provision that special panels would decide whether U.S. trade laws were being correctly applied. But even if a panel were to rule against the U.S., the U.S. would be free to change its laws unilaterally to negate such a ruling.

Before the free trade era, Canada was able to oppose U.S. charges that its agricultural supports and its regional development and transportation programs were "trade-distorting," but under the free trade deals disputes in each of these cases were settled in favour of the U.S.

**Agriculture:** The experience of Canadian farmers clearly demonstrates that more trade does not necessarily translate into more prosperity. The National Farmers Union points out that, since 1988, agricultural exports have almost tripled, but net farm income (adjusted for inflation) has fallen by 24%. Over the same period, farm debt has doubled, 16% of Canadian farmers have been forced off the land, the number of independent hog farmers has dropped by 66%, and there are 2,400 fewer jobs in the agri-food processing industry.

The NFU concludes that free trade agreements "may increase trade, but they dramatically alter the relative size and market power of the players in the agri-food production chain. Free trade helps Cargill and Monsanto, not farmers."

**Social inequality:** Canada has become a noticeably more unequal society in the free trade era. Real incomes declined for most Canadians in the 1990s, with median income in 1999 having dropped by $1,100, or 2%, from the 1990 level. While this decline can't entirely be blamed on free trade, it is undeniable that the downward pressure on wages, the loss of so many secure full-time jobs, and the sharp cutbacks to social transfer payments have contributed significantly to rising inequality.

Free trade and other neoliberal economic policies have also led to a markedly more unequal distribution of wealth. From 1984 to 1999, the poorest 40% of Canadians had their share of the nation's total wealth reduced from 1.8% of all personal assets to just 1.1%. Over the same period, the richest 10% of the population enjoyed a rise in net worth from 51.8% of all wealth to 55.7%.

## The United States

The proponents of NAFTA in the United States claimed that it would create more jobs through increased exports, and that these jobs would provide good wages and benefits. They further predicted that the economic growth generated by free trade would promote economic equality and a reduction of poverty. Higher rates of productivity, they added, would enhance American workers' living standards, and special side-agreements would protect the environment and labour rights.

Now, 10 years later, none of these claims has materialized. In fact, the exact opposite has occurred. We don't allege that all the economic problems we cite below have been caused by NAFTA alone, but we believe that NAFTA has made them worse. More importantly, NAFTA is now only one part—albeit a crucial part—of a global "free trade" structure that glorifies the workings of a deregulated market, demonizes government planning and regulation, and perceives human beings and civil society generally as little more than customers in a vast continental shopping mall.

Canada and Mexico are the United States' No. 1 and No. 2 trade partners in terms of the volume of exports. Together, they constitute 39% of all U.S. trade activity, and their importance is even greater when we consider the volume of capital flows within North America.

So we need to look both specifically at the impacts of trade and investment flows on the U.S., and also whether, after 10 years of NAFTA, this model of free trade is living up to the promises its proponents have made. If their promises have not been kept, as we believe to be the case, it is high time to consider alternatives.

**NAFTA and employment:** The exact number of U.S. workers negatively affected by NAFTA is difficult to calculate. A special Act of Congress created a program of benefits for workers who have been certified as having lost jobs due to NAFTA, and, as of July 2002, the number stood at 413,123. But this figure grossly understates the job losses directly caused by NAFTA because many workers don't know about this program and others apply for relief under a more generic trade adjustment program. Also pertinent is that only industrial workers can qualify. Service providers are not eligible, nor are workers who lose their jobs indirectly to NAFTA such as auto parts suppliers who are laid off when the auto plant they serve is moved to Mexico. Thus the number of jobs lost directly and indirectly because of NAFTA is considerably higher than 413,123.

U.S. employment did grow during the late 1990s, but that growth served mainly to redistribute employment into industries that pay lower wages and offer fewer benefits. This shift is perceptible in the fact that, between 1990 and 2000, manufacturing industries in the U.S. lost 1.5 million jobs. Meanwhile, service sector employment grew by 10.5 million jobs, and retail and wholesale trade jobs increased by 3 million. Service sector jobs accounted for 99% of the net new jobs created during the 1990s. Surveys of such displaced industrial workers indicate that they suffered a reduction of wages of 13%, on average, when they found new employment in the service sector. Average wages in the service sector are only 77% of those in manufacturing.

**NAFTA and labour:** During the NAFTA debate, unions feared its impact on worker rights. The Clinton administration responded with a weak side agreement designed to gain some labour support. But this side agreement is so toothless and cumbersome that it has never effectively protected the rights of workers. As the unions feared, the greater ease afforded the corporations to move operations out of the U.S. has armed them with the threat of moving to undermine job security and quality, suppress wages, and discourage union organizing. When firms actually do move, jobs are lost—not because of increased competition from Canadian and Mexican imports, but because of the availability of lower wages elsewhere.

Studies have found that, between 1992 and 1995, over half the employers surveyed had used the threat of closing and/or moving production during union organizing drives, and to resist union bargaining efforts if such drives were successful. The average annual number of new union members gained through organizing efforts dropped from about 300,000 in the mid-1970s to less than 100,000 by the mid-1990s.

NAFTA proponents claimed that the higher rates of productivity spurred by free trade would protect U.S. workers' living standards. Productivity indeed increased during the 1990s, but wages relative to this productivity growth have lost considerable ground. While productivity rose by 25% between 1990 and 2000, real wage growth was only 8%. Thus, in an era of high capital mobility and falling unionization, the relationship of wages to productivity has come apart—and the result has been a lower living standard for U.S. workers.

The stagnation of wages and the shift in the distribution of jobs has contributed to a significant redistribution of income from the poor and middle income groups to those in the higher income brackets. During the 1990s, the richest 5% of the population increased their share of total family income in the U.S. by nearly 3%, while the poorest 20% lost about 4% of their share.

The spillover effects of these NAFTA-induced changes include a decline in the number of workers covered by health care benefits as they were shifted into jobs without such benefits; a sharp increase in part-time, temporary, on-call, and other forms of contingent work; increases in the rates of poverty and homelessness; and rising rates of incarceration.

The shift in jobs to lower wage areas has not only depressed wages in the U.S., but has also created a global system of production in which goods are produced by the cheapest labour. Some economists have argued that this system is more "efficient," but it has also reduced the ability of consumers to buy the products of the cheap-wage system. During the 1990s, this slack was taken up by a large increase in consumer debt—up from 63% of annual personal income in 1979 to 85% in 1997. Between 1990 and 2000, credit card debt grew from $432 billion to $1,173 billion.

This level of consumer debt has acted as a drag on economic recovery in the U.S., and so has the debt incurred by the growing negative balance of trade. Spending more on imports than exports in the U.S. as a whole has meant that during the 1990s the U.S. has had to borrow money from outside the country to make up the difference. Specifically, we have been accumulating a debt with the rest of the world that amounts to 23% of our GDP, which is over $400 billion a year—a figure that some economists predict will balloon to 40% by 2006.

**NAFTA and Immigration:** One of the promises of NAFTA was that it would help Mexico and lower pressures to immigrate to the U.S. This has not happened. Between 1991 and 2000, the number of persons declared "illegal aliens" and deported from the U.S. grew by 51% to 1,814,729, with 95% of these deportees being from Mexico. Between 1998 and 2001, legal Mexican immigration to the U.S. increased by 40%, and in 2001 205,000 Mexicans came to this country. Violations of the civil rights of Mexican migrants to the United States are a growing problem, both when they attempt to cross the border and once they are living and working in the United States.

**NAFTA and Inequality:** The problems associated with NAFTA and other trade agreements have exacerbated inequalities between people of colour and white society. The gap in wages between white workers and those of both African Americans and Latinos has widened. In 1990, the difference between white median family income and that of African Americans and Latinos was $12,645 and $18,901, respectively. By 2000, these gaps had increased to $14,249 and $19,748.

There is also a gap in access to health care benefits that has not been narrowed in the NAFTA years. In 2000, 67% of whites received health care benefits, compared with 60% of African Americans and 45% of Latinos.

One reason for these growing gaps has to do with the massive job dislocation that has been caused by negative trade balances and highly mobile capital. African Americans and Latinos are often the first to be laid off and it takes them longer to find alternative employment. As a result, unemployment rates of both African Americans and Latinos have been consistently higher during the 1990-2000 period. In 1990, the African American employment rate was three times higher than the rate for whites (15.1% compared to 4.8%). Latinos had a rate of 9.3%. By 2000, with strong economic growth, the gaps narrowed slightly but were still significant—7.6% for African Americans and 5.7% for Latinos, compared with a rate of 3.5% for whites. So even in the best of times these minority groups did poorly, and during the current recession it is likely that the gaps will widen once more.

The end result is that more African Americans and Latinos have fallen into poverty and/or have been incarcerated. The average poverty rate for whites between 1999 and 2000 was 7.5%, but for African Americans was 23.1% and for Latinos 22.1%. At present, African Americans and Latinos make up 62% of the U.S. prison population. In 1999, 11% of all black males and 4% of Latinos in their 20s and 30s were in prison or jail, compared with only 1.5% of whites in the same age bracket.

## Mexico

The government of Mexico regarded NAFTA as a fundamental element in its overall economic strategy. This strategy was—and continues to be—the IMF and World Bank recipe: growth based on exports and the stimulus of foreign investment. Proponents of NAFTA promised that it would generate more jobs and reduce poverty. Mexican exports did indeed grow enormously, and there was a huge inflow of foreign investment—but no significant economic growth was achieved, and neither more nor better jobs were created.

The Mexican government and the country's largest economic players have promoted NAFTA as a success. They cite data which, although accurate, are much too general and serve mainly to hide the deep problems that still plague the economy. These "success" stories have been repeated so often that they have become myths, leading people not to question or analyze them, but rather to support the extension of NAFTA to the rest of the hemisphere in the proposed Free Trade Area of the Americas (FTAA).

But it is imperative to evaluate the results of NAFTA before approving it blindly as a model for other countries.

**Foreign trade:** Exports increased by over 300% under NAFTA, from US$51.9 million in 1993 to $160.7 million in 2002. During the first nine years of NAFTA, Mexico's accumulated exports exceeded a trillion dollars ($1,086,285,300,000). These exports were mainly manufactured goods. Since the inception of NAFTA, Mexico has built up a $141 billion accumulated trade surplus with the United States.

These spectacular figures feed a myth—that Mexico has become the No. 1 exporter in Latin America and one of the leading exporters in the world, and that this is all due to NAFTA. It is a purported success story that is presented to other Latin American countries as a strong argument for them to negotiate and sign the FTAA. But a more careful analysis of the export data exposes a far different—and far less bright—reality.

Clearly, the objective should be not just to export, but to export in order to grow and create jobs. Paradoxically, these enormous foreign sales have not been translated into growth in the Mexican economy. The average annual rate of per capita growth of its GDP under NAFTA has been less than 1%. The trade surplus with the U.S. is mainly due to *maquiladora* and petroleum production, whose dynamics are independent of NAFTA. And much of the trade surplus takes the form of intra-firm trade among U.S. companies. Three of the largest five export companies in Mexico are U.S. automotive plants that assemble cars in Mexico in order to sell them globally, with many going to the U.S. The same is true with computer assembly plants. Mexico exports many other industrial products to the U.S., but the manufacturing sector as a whole is running a trade *deficit*.

So it is an exaggeration to say that Mexico has become a manufacturing export power because of NAFTA. In reality, in the NAFTA period, 54% of exports have been petroleum or *maquiladora* production
—and these exports have not generated general growth in the Mexican economy. Also significant is that most of the inputs in Mexico's exports are imported goods.

The Mexican economic strategy is based on the idea that exports will be an engine of growth for the economy, but that has not happened, mainly because the export companies are not connected to the rest of the country through national productive linkages. Instead, they are like an island that is disconnected from the rest of the economy and generating hardly any new jobs.

As for the foreign investment, it is concentrated predominantly in these export-oriented companies. Five of the six biggest export firms are 100% foreign owned and account for more than 20% of total exports. In summary, Mexico exports a lot, but what it exports is nor very Mexican, and the increase in exports spurred by NAFTA has not been an engine of economic growth, nor has it generated the promised additional jobs.

**NAFTA's real purpose:** Under the NAFTA rules on trade and investment, conditions are created so that companies find it easier to maximize their profits, but without any requirement to contribute to the host country's development. In an export-oriented economy, under NAFTA, the interests of the exporting country are ignored. A foreign company can set up Mexico and produce goods for export in a way that does little or nothing to promote overall economic or employment growth.

To overcome these problems, a country needs a well-defined national industrial policy, but the terms of NAFTA put severe limits on developing any such policy, leaving everything instead to market forces. The upshot is that, without any industrial policy, accelerated trade liberalization has pulled the Mexican economy into a vicious tug-of-war between growth and trade deficit, to the "denationalization" of its exports and the delinking of national production chains. The advocates of NAFTA claim that it generates modernization, efficiency, and competitiveness. This is the basis for the theory of free trade, but its failure to accomplish any of these things in Mexico exposes the theory as a myth.

**Foreign investment:** Direct investment in Mexico has increased under NAFTA—totalling some US$153 billion up to 2002—but it is not well integrated into the country's national productive chains and therefore has not produced the promised multiplier effects in terms of growth and employment. It has been mainly concentrated in the manufacturing export sector, in banking, and in commerce. There was virtually no foreign investment in the Mexican countryside, just a bare 0.25% during the entire NAFTA period. So the gap between Mexico's poor and marginalized areas and those that enjoy greater wealth has been widened by NAFTA, not narrowed.

**Employment:** The negotiators and promoters of NAFTA promised that it would create more and better jobs. They now speak of "thousands" of jobs having been generated by the export sector. There is no doubt that large exporters and the *maquiladoras* have hired more workers, but conversely, many jobs have been lost by the former domestic suppliers to those exporters.

During the first nine years of NAFTA, 8,073,201 new jobs were created in the country—but that number was 46.6% *lower* than was needed to provide work for all the people aged 15-64 entering the workforce. In addition, most of these new jobs were "bad" jobs, with 55% of them not providing even the minimal benefits required by law, such as social security, 10 days' vacation a year, and a Christmas bonus. These are general data, of course, and are influenced by many factors besides NAFTA, but they do demonstrate the failure of the country's basic economic strategy—of which NAFTA is a key element—to generate growth and employment.

Productivity has increased by 53% in the non-*maquiladora* manufacturing sector during the NAFTA years, which would be a welcome improvement if the benefits of the higher productivity were shared with the workers. But in fact, during the nine years of NAFTA, labour costs (mainly wages and benefits) *declined* by 36%—meaning that the workers produced 53% more per hour of work, but at a 36% less cost for employers. NAFTA's impact on the agricultural sector is even more dramatic than critics had predicted. Imports of corn and oilseeds have increased from 8.8 million metric tons a year in 1993 to 20.3 million metric tons in 2002. The situation with meat, tropical fruits and other products is similar. These imports have replaced national products, increasing rural unemployment. Statistics indicate that Mexico is losing its food sovereignty and instead has increased its dependency on imports, which has generated a major outflow of foreign currency. The supposed advantages for consumers based on greater access to less expensive, imported food products turned out to be pure rhetoric. From 1994 to 2002, the prices the goods in the basic food basket increased 257 percent, while prices paid to agricultural producers rose only 185 percent.

Trade relations between Mexico and the United States and Canada are characterized by numerous inequalities that explain much of NAFTA's negative impact on the agricultural sector. These include asymmetries existing even before NAFTA, such as differences in levels of technology and higher production costs for energy and other inputs, problems in the negotiations, including Mexico's failure to exclude sensitive agricultural goods and the lack of any provisions to review the accord, and problems after the signing of the agreement, particularly the passage of the 2002 US Farm Bill, which dramatically expanded the already unequal levels of subsidies given to U.S. farmers.

Organizations of small, medium and business-level producers representing the great majority of the country's farmers have united in the "El Campo No Aguanta Más" (The Countryside Can't Take It Anymore) campaign. They are calling for the suspension of NAFTA, or at least for its renegotiation, because less than a thousand individuals have come out ahead as a result of NAFTA, while millions are on the losing end.

## An issue for all: NAFTA's Chapter 11

This "investor-state" clause gives foreign investors the right to sue governments directly for compensation for immediate or even future loss of profits caused by public interest laws. Chapter 11 is a serious threat to the ability of governments at all levels to pass laws or adopt policies that serve the public good.

Corporations seeking damages under the investor-state clause can take their claims to special NAFTA tribunals, whose hearings are usually held in secret, with no obligation to allow participation by private citizens, NGOs, or even local government officials. Such tribunals supersede the authority of national courts—and their rulings cannot be appealed.

So far, 27 charges by corporations against governments have been filed under Chapter 11. Both the Canadian and U.S. governments have been sued over bans on hazardous gasoline additives. The Canadian government settled the case involving MMT, a nerve toxin, by paying the U.S.-based Ethyl Corporation $13 million in compensation. Canada's Methanex Corporation is demanding $970 million in compensation for a California ban on MTBE, a chemical that can cause cancer that was leaching into local groundwater. The U.S. Metalclad Company successfully sued Mexico over a local community's refusal to allow the company to open a toxic-waste dump without the necessary environmental precautions. In each of these cases, the public danger posed by the banned chemicals or environmental conditions was not a consideration, only the companies' loss of actual or potential profits.

There is also evidence that companies are using the threat of investor-state charges to discourage governments from even

considering the passage of new public-interest laws. Lobbyists for the U.S. tobacco giants Philip Morris and R.J. Reynolds threatened such a suit when the Canadian government proposed to legislate plain packaging for cigarettes, and the legislation was quickly withdrawn.
Similar threats in recent years have reportedly scuttled planned Canadian environmental and public-safety laws on pesticides, pharmaceuticals, and other chemicals.

Despite the inhibiting effects of Chapter 11, however, none of the three NAFTA governments has tried to eliminate or even modify this clause. On the contrary, their efforts continue to extend it to other countries in the hemisphere through the proposed FTAA.

## Conclusion

NAFTA has not fulfilled the objectives and expectations set forth by its promoters. It has not even achieved significant economic growth—at least, not stable, sustained and sustainable growth. And it certainly has not brought social justice.

Even the low growth rate that has occurred has come at the cost of massive environmental degradation and the depletion of natural resources.

Instead of creating more and better jobs, NAFTA has accelerated the disintegration of national production chains and the denationalization of the country's productive structure. Nearly all the banks in Mexico and most of the large export companies are now owned by foreigners.

There have been few winners and many losers. NAFTA has created a few islands of economic success—very successful in terms of profits for their owners and investors—but the economy as a whole has not benefited.

Taking stock of these results of NAFTA should lead to a rethinking of the way that Mexico has been integrated into the global economy. Clearly, NAFTA is not a model that other countries should emulate. No country's welfare should ever be left solely to market forces. A viable national development plan is essential—one that allows a country to create the economic conditions that will optimize its economic potential.

We do not need more free trade agreements. We do not need deregulation and unfettered competition. We need international agreements that promote sustainable development and a more equitable distribution of income at both the national and global levels.

Another world is possible. So is another and better form of globalization.

# Introduction
## by Alberto Arroyo Picard

When the leaders of Canada, the United States and Mexico signed the North American Free Trade Agreement (NAFTA) in 1993, its proponents heralded it not just as an agreement to lower barriers to trade in goods, but as a tool for increased economic growth and strengthened democracy. The following country case studies, prepared by members of national civil-society networks in the three countries, demonstrate that the concrete results have been much different. Before entering into an objective analysis of the results the agreement, however, it is important to clarify our networks' position on globalization.

We do not believe in isolated economies, nor are we nostalgic for the past. We fully understand that no country can remain isolated from the world economy. We should integrate into the world economy and market, but there is no one way to achieve that goal and we do not believe that free trade is either the only or the best way of doing so. We believe that integration should start from a national development plan. That plan should consider conditions in the world market, but not just to accept them passively, but rather to seek in them the conditions to advance the national plan. Negotiations should not remove all regulations and leave the global market to shape our countries through free trade agreements. To the contrary, we should negotiate rules for the world economy that ensure sustainability and the viability of just development for our countries, i.e., agreements for just and sustainable development. The Hemispheric Social Alliance, of which our networks are members, has presented a comprehensive proposal along these lines.[1]

We do not believe that other countries should always refuse to negotiate with the United States. Historically, both Canada and Mexico have the majority of their trade with that country, and it is the source of the majority of their foreign investment. In principle, it was a good idea to formalize the rules of that relationship. Before NAFTA, trade relations between Mexico and the US were based on the rules in the Generalized System of Preferences, which were unilaterally defined by the United States and changed constantly, so it was useful to enter into discussions on more stable rules developed through a multilateral process. The problem lies in the orientation with which that agreement was negotiated and the concrete rules agreed upon.

It is important to take into account that NAFTA is much more than an agreement on trade liberalization. It goes far beyond the rules in the World Trade Organization (WTO) to include provisions on many issues that are only now beginning to be discussed in the WTO, issues such as investment, energy, role of the state and government procurement. NAFTA treats the service sector more thoroughly than the WTO and it includes rules on the entire agricultural sector, which no developed country has ever completely liberalized.

NAFTA was yet another step in the extension of neoliberal policies, which were first imposed on many countries through the conditions attached to World Bank and International Monetary Fund structural adjustment agreements. Those institutions hold enormous power over underdeveloped countries that have periodically entered into debt payment crises. Those countries could only renegotiate their loans if they had the IMF's blessing, which it did not give unless countries signed Letters of Intent agreeing to implement economic strategies and measures to reorient production to export and the private sector, leaving economic planning to market forces.

The experiences of the 1990s, however, demonstrated the limits of that approach. In the first place, the economic successes of the "Asian Tigers" did not emerge from Bank and Fund recipe. They were able to chart their own course in large part because they did not have unpayable foreign debts. The case of

Mexico demonstrates another limitation. Salinas lost the 1988 presidential elections and had to impose himself through fraud. What would happen if the leaders who support neoliberalism begin to lose power due to the discontent arising from the impoverishment created by this model? Both of these issues made world economic powers think that they had to do something to ensure the continuity of this economic strategy. The new piece is free-trade agreements.

In essence, trade and investment agreements are designed to convert the neoliberal model into supranational law and therefore to establish a kind of insurance against democratic changes. Renato Ruggiero, the former General Director of the World Trade Organization could not have expressed it better when he said that the negotiation of international investment agreements is like "writing the constitution of a single world economy". That is to say, a kind of "constitution" in the legal sense of the word, that guarantees rights to investors with practically no obligations. These agreements delimit what governments can and cannot do. In the future, fundamental decisions on our countries' economic policy and strategy will not be developed in each country's democratic institutions; they will be set by supranational law.

The official discourse often associates free trade with democracy. In reality, nearly all countries have elections and formal democracy. But free-trade agreements set the broad orientations for economic policies in supranational law and they drastically reduce elected officials' ability to influence and orient economic dynamics according to the interests of the majority of the population. Democracy and elections have less and less to do with people's economic lives, with standards of living, with the possibility of obtaining employment, with maintaining the right to health, to education, etc, as those issues are not decided by elected officials.

Free-trade agreements are based on an economic theory that assumes that everything will work better if left to market forces. These agreements do not just liberalize foreign trade; they are designed to eliminate all government regulation or intervention in the market. They are not negotiated starting from a national development plan, but rather based on the idea, as expressed by Dr. Herminio Blanco, the chief Mexican negotiator, "the best national plan is not to have a national plan and to let the market shape the best Mexico possible." This theory has no historical backing. In no country in the world has the market alone achieved sustainability and social justice.

The following articles demonstrate that NAFTA has failed to deliver on its proponents' promises to increase economic growth, to create more and better jobs and to strengthen democracy in the region. It has been devastating for many people in all three countries and has lead to increased pressure on Canada and Mexico to conform to U.S. foreign policy goals. Most alarmingly, the three governments are working to extend this failed model throughout the Americas in the proposed Free Trade Area of the Americas. Before leaping into that abyss, citizens and policymakers throughout the hemisphere should stop and look at the concrete results of this model for corporate-led globalization.

# Chapter 1
# NAFTA in Mexico: Promises, Myths and Realities
## by Alberto Arroyo Picard[2]

The Mexican government regarded NAFTA as a fundamental element in its overall economic strategy. The strategy was and continues to be exactly the IMF and World Bank recipe: growth based on the attraction of foreign demand (exports) and the stimulus of foreign investment. According to the proponents of that model, the resulting growth would then generate jobs and reduce poverty. In fact, Mexican exports grew enormously, and a huge inflow of foreign investment, including direct investment, entered the country, but no significant growth was achieved and neither more nor better jobs were created. An explanation must be sought for these paradoxical results.

We present in this essay an evaluation of the macroeconomic results of nine years of NAFTA in Mexico. We will do so in the form of contrasts. On the one hand, there are the promises made during the negotiating process and the current claims made by the proponents for the Free Trade Area of the Americas (FTAA), and, on the other hand, the hard reality of evidence. The necessary brevity of this report requires concentrating on a few issues, but they were not chosen just to present a negative image. They are the fundamental issues that follow from the objectives proposed by the promoters of NAFTA and now the FTAA.[3]

The Mexican government and the largest economic interests in the country promoted NAFTA as a success based on certain data, which, although true, are much too general and hide deep problems in the Mexican economy. These "success" stories have been repeated so often they have become myths. This myth leads people not to question or analyze, to uncritically follow the same economic strategy, and to support the negotiation of more and more agreements under the same criteria as NAFTA. The social problems are acknowledged, but there is no will to see that they are intimately connected to the economic strategy, or at least that the strategy is not helping to diminish them.

We believe that there must be a profound and objective evaluation of the results of the treaty in order to have the necessary information to rethink the way Mexico is integrating into the world economy. It is also imperative to evaluate the results of NAFTA before continuing the negotiations for the FTAA or other similar accords.

Four issues are presented in this paper: foreign trade; foreign investment; economic growth; and employment. The first three are at the heart of the Mexican economic strategy, within which NAFTA was negotiated and the fourth is the social issue most directly connected to macroeconomic issues.

# I. Foreign Trade

### 1. Presumed successes
- Exports increased just over 300 percent during NAFTA. Exports (including maquiladora production) grew from US$51.886 million in 1993 to US$160.682 million in 2002. During the nine years since NAFTA's inception, Mexico's accumulated exports surpassed a trillion dollars (US$1,086,285,300,000)[4];
- These exports were mainly manufactured goods. On average, during NAFTA 87.35 percent of exports were manufactured goods (including maquiladora production). Dependence on oil exports was thus overcome. Before NAFTA, Mexico was a primary products exporter, selling mainly agricultural and mineral goods abroad. In the 1970s, crude oil comprised the majority of its exports. In 1981 petroleum amounted to 72.5 percent of exports, while by 2002

it was just 9 percent, which was also the average figure during the nine years of NAFTA.[5]

- Since NAFTA's inception, Mexico has a US$141 billion accumulated trade surplus with the United States.[6]

These spectacular data feed a myth, that Mexico has become the number one exporter in Latin American and one of the principal exporters in the world and that this is all due to NAFTA. The path Mexico followed is presented to the rest of the hemisphere as a strong argument to invite them to negotiate and sign the FTAA. These three visible achievements, however, analyzed in greater depth, demonstrate more complex and negative realities.

### 2. Reality demonstrates the failure of this strategy

Clearly, the objective is not just to export, but to export in order to grow and create jobs. Paradoxically, these enormous foreign sales did not translate into growth in the Mexican economy. As demonstrated later in this paper, the average rate of growth of GDP per capita was less than one percent. We must analyze the date on foreign trade in greater depth in order to find the explanation for this paradox.

a) Foreign trade continues to mean the exit of money from the country. Mexico has signed numerous free-trade treaties. From 1994 to December 2002 it accumulated a US$43.67 billion trade deficit with the rest of the world[7] and a US$121.36 billion current account deficit.[8]

b) The trade surplus with the United States is mainly due to petroleum and maquiladora production, whose dynamics are independent of NAFTA. Petroleum exports really haven't increased significantly. Prior to NAFTA (1988-1993), average daily exports were 1.37 million barrels and during NAFTA (1994-2002) they were 1.47 million barrels a day. The volume of petroleum exports increased just 7.26 percent. This kind of exports responded to demand and did not depend on the NAFTA rules. Sales of crude petroleum in the Americas during the NAFTA years totaled US$75.502 million, which accounted for 55 percent of the trade deficit with the United States[9]. Maquilador exports did increase during this period, but not because of NAFTA. In reality, the advantages established under the maquiladora program did not improve under NAFTA; instead they were extended to the economy as a whole. Official statistics do not separate maquiladora exports by country, but at least 90 percent is to the United States. There is a US$105.7 billion trade surplus in the maquiladora sector. If 90 percent of that is to the United States, that would be US$95.160, that is, 67.5 percent of the trade surplus with the United States[10]. The total of maquiladora and petroleum exports is 22.5 percent more than the trade surplus with that country.

Another important element of the trade surplus with the United States is intra-firm trade among U.S. companies. There are no aggregate public statistics on this issue, but the second, third and fifth largest export companies from Mexico are three U.S. automotive plants that assemble cars in Mexico in order to sell them globally, with many of them going to the United States. This is also the case with computer assembly, where Hewlett Packard is the sixth largest exporter in the country. Mexico exports many other industrial products to the United States, but the manufacturing sector as a whole has a trade deficit[11].

Moreover, the trade surplus with the United States is not unusual in Mexico's recent history. Before NAFTA, under full trade liberalization, there was a surplus between 1985 and 1990. The exception was during the Salinas Administration (1991-1994), when there was a deficit. Another important fact demonstrating that NAFTA does not explain the trade surplus is that Mexico has a trade deficit with Canada. During the nine years before NAFTA, Mexico had a US$667 million trade surplus, and during the NAFTA period Mexico had a US$3.739 billion deficit with that country.[12]

These two elements clearly indicate that it is an exaggeration to speak of Mexico as a manufacturing export power. In reality, during NAFTA, 54.35 percent of exports are petroleum or maquiladora production. But the most important fact is that these exports have not translated into general growth in the economy. We will explore some of the characteristics of Mexican exports that explain this paradox.

c) The majority of the inputs in Mexico's exports are imported goods. The maquiladora industry is an extreme case: on average during the NAFTA years, that industry bought just 2.97 percent of its components and packaging in the country[13]. If labor is included, the total for 1996 was just 17 percent[14]. In 1983, the non-maquiladora manufacturing sector had 91 percent national content, but by 1996 that figure had fallen to just 37 percent.[15] That is to say, Mexico exported a lot, but nearly all of the components of those exports are imported goods.

The Mexican economic strategy is based on the idea that exports will be an engine of growth for the economy, but that has not been the case, since the export companies are not connected to the rest of the economy through national productive linkages; they are a kind of island disconnected from the rest of the economy. They produce almost no effect on the rest of the economy and do not generate jobs.

d) Foreign investment is concentrated in precisely those export-oriented companies. Some 49.5 percent of direct foreign investment goes to manufacturing[16], which, as described above, is where exports are concentrated. Five of the six biggest export companies are 100 percent foreign owned and represent more than 20 percent of total exports[17].

In summary, Mexico exports a lot but what it exports is not very Mexican, both in term of its owners and its components. This could be the most profoundly negative macroeconomic impact of NAFTA: the disintegration of productive linkages and the de-nationalization of the productive structure.

e)   In conclusion, Mexico exports a lot, but it is not an export power, and above all the strategy has not worked since these exports have not been an engine of economic growth. Growth and the trade surplus have not been reconciled. When the Mexican economy grows, it has large trade deficits with the world, which means that the more the economy grows, the more resources leave the country. As demonstrated in the following table, Mexico's trade surplus with the world is intimately related to periods of recession or stagnation in the economy.

### 3. The relationship between these results and what was negotiated in NAFTA

But what does NAFTA have to do with these poor results? It is true that many of the problems indicated here occurred

**Table 1-1**
**Trade Balance and Growth (Millions of Dollars)**

| Year | | Trade Balance Average w/maquila | Avg. Rate Incr in GDP | deficit/each Point GDP |
|---|---|---|---|---|
| 1970-1981 | DEFICIT | (1,991.3) | 6.87% | (289.8) |
| 1982-1988 | SURPLUS | 8,398.6 | 0.19% | |
| 1989-1994 | DEFICIT | (9,272.2) | 3.90% | (2,377.5) |
| 1995-1997 | SURPLUS | 4,747.7 | 1.73% | |
| 1998-2002 | DEFICIT | (8,766.5) | 3.13% | (2,800.8) |

**Sources: Trade Balance** 1970-1980 Banco de México Tomado del Anexo al **III Informe de Gobierno de Carlos Salinas de Gortari (CSG)** p. 201. There are methodological changes so it is not possible to compare before and after 1980. 1981-1985 Banco de México. Taken from Anexo **VI Informe de Gobierno CSG** P. 140. 1986-1988 Banco de México tomado del **II Inf. de Gob. Ernesto Zedillo Ponce de León (EZPL)** Pág. 95. 1988-1997 Grupo de trabajo INEGI, SHCP, Banco de Méx. Tomado Anexo **V inf. EZPL** Pág. 113. 1998...Grupo de trabajo INEGI, SHCP, Banco de Méx. Tomado de web SHCP www.shcp.gob.mx **Average rate of increase in GDP** * Up to 1981 calculated from a series in 1980 pesos. Taken from INEGI-BIE. (Estadísticas de la Contabilidad Nacional/ PIB por Gran división, división y rama de actividad económica). Date from 1981 forward taken from a series in 1993 pesos. Quarterly GDP in 1993 prices/by division of economic activity/absolute values/total. Taken from de INEGI-BIE. All data to December 2002.

before NAFTA and that they have multiple causes. However, NAFTA clearly did not help to minimize them. We will see shortly how what was agreed to in NAFTA not only did not help to overcome these problems in the Mexican economy, but worsened them.

a)  The rules of origin agreed to in NAFTA do not favor increases in domestic content of exports, since they only require North American regional, not national content. The name "rules of origin" would seem to indicate a requirement that goods contain a certain percentage of inputs made in the country that exports them. But that is not the case, the only requirement is content from the North American region.[18] Under these rules, intra-firm or consortium integration is facilitated, helping large consortia to integrate their own productive chains. These rules do not favor the integration of the Mexican economy into the global dynamic.

b)  It is said that export companies do not purchase from Mexican businesses because of the lack of competitiveness of our industries, but that is not always so. There are cases that document the opposite.

The "Rubestos" company, which produces brake lining, sold most of its brake lining to Volkswagon Mexico. One day the order was cancelled. After months of attempting to learn the reason, a Volkswagon official confessed that Rubestos' brake linings were better quality and lower in price than what they were now buying, but "there is no better business than to buy from yourself" (VW has brake lining plants in many other parts of the world). This businessman decided to enter a niche market in which he thought he would have no problems. He oriented his production to produce special brake lining (made to order) for the tire industry. However, one day they stopped buying from him. This seemed strange since large brake lining plants have little flexibility to produce specially sized linings. He looked into what had happened and discovered that some U.S. tire factories had simply decided not to purchase in Mexico. In neither of these cases was the Mexican manufacturer given the opportunity to compete.[19]

In reality, the terms negotiated in NAFTA are an important factor in the low Mexican content. Export companies are not required to submit their purchases for bids as they would be if they were government agencies or state-owned enterprises. Mexican companies often don't even have the opportunity to compete. In reality, the large transnational firms promoted free-trade agreements to facilitate their own intra-firm integration without having to comply with various requirements or standards set by each country's legislators. Neoliberal globalization seeks the integration of the different parts of large transnational corporations, not the integration of the countries in which they operate in the world economic system. If this were to be truly consistent with free trade and competition theory, there would have to be mechanisms in NAFTA that would require bids on large purchases, but that was only agreed to for purchases by the public sector. It is paradoxical that these rules oblige the public sector to submit all of its purchases and important works for bidding, which therefore impedes their using those purchases or investments as party of an economic policy that supports the development of national industry and that the same conditions do not apply to large corporations. If competition leads to lower prices and that favors consumers, why do large corporations not put their purchases for bids and make their suppliers compete? The truth is that the real objective is not competition that benefits the consumer, but maximizing private profits and for that reason, companies prefer to buy from themselves.

c) In addition, NAFTA and the FTAA negotiations serve to ratify those rules, practically prohibiting demanding performance requirements or rules of conduct for foreign investors. Under these conditions, the state cannot establish policies to ensure that foreign investment plays a positive role in national development and the population's welfare. Under the NAFTA rules on trade and investment, conditions are created so that companies maximize their profits, but without the requirement of any quid pro quo in terms of contributing to the country's development.

d) In this negotiation, the interests of the exporting country do not matter at all. A company can come and carry out in Mexico those functions that require more labor and then export and sell in the United States or Canada. The least one can say is that these terms do not help exports to become engines of growth and employment generation.

e) Confronting the problems described above implies a defined national industrial policy and NAFTA puts extreme limits on the possibility of leading a national development plan. Instead, it leaves everything to market forces.[20]

f) Accelerated trade liberalization without any industrial policy has led the Mexican economy into a vicious circle between growth and trade deficit, to the denationalization of our exports and the delinking of national production chains. Trade liberalization alone does not generate competitiveness in national businesses, it only penalizes with death those that do not achieve it. What was negotiated in NAFTA worsens this problem.

It is often asserted that trade liberalization generates modernization, efficiency and competitiveness. This myth is the basis for the theory of free trade.

We will not attempt now to expose the discussion of that theory. We have already said that there is much more involved in an economic strategy than simply proposing open markets. This theory maintains that the market is the best regulator of the economy, that by itself, if it is not disturbed, if it is left "free", it guarantees the best possible distribution of resources and benefits. This, taken to the international level, maintains that there should be no national development plans, that the best results will be achieved by the market if all obstacles to the world market are removed.

No one denies that the market is competition and that competitions demands efficiency. But the market and competition do not produce efficiency, they only demand it. The market is only the test; much must be done to survive and win in it. Trade liberalization was supposed to make the Mexican economy compete in the big leagues, but the necessary industrial policy to arrive that market under competitive conditions was not carried out. Even worse, the NAFTA rules unreasonably limit the possibilities for an active role of the state in the economy to implement a defined and active industrial policy.

It is not that the Mexican economy should close again. The previous model, called stabilizing development, implied exaggerated protectionism whose defects led to its exhaustion. There was no definite time limit set for the protection, it was indiscriminate, and the development and support policy suffered from numerous inconsistencies. The evaluation of this protection policy should recognize the mistakes, learn from them, but in no way lead to the rejection of any kind of protection. The experience of the past indicates that protection should not be generalized, if some sectors should be protected, that should be planned, with a defined time period, and with support conditioned on evaluations against pre-established goals.

In Mexico there has not been a deep evaluation of the import substitution model, there was simply a change to the other extreme, with almost indiscriminate and accelerated liberalization of the economy to international competition. It was not accompanied by an industrial and financial policy. Dr. Herminio Blanco, the former Secretary of Commerce, asserted that the best industrial policy was not to have an industrial policy. In other words, the industrial policy was simply to make the productive structure compete.

It is true that the necessary efforts to arrive at the market under competitive conditions should be in large part the responsibility of the economic actors themselves. But the state should not renounce its responsibility to generate adequate general conditions. It should direct the liberalization starting from a long-term national plan.

## II. Foreign Investment

From NAFTA's inception to 2002, US$152.83 billion entered the country as foreign investment. The annual average was US$16.98 billion. This amount is very similar to the average for the five years prior to NAFTA (US$16.56 billion). It is positive that most of this, some 79.34 percent or US$121.26 billion, is direct foreign investment, while in the five years prior to NAFTA, just 23.38 percent was direct investment[21].

This change in composition and the fat that the majority is direct foreign investment is important. Some US$3.87 billion in direct investment entered the country in the five years prior to NAFTA, while during the nine years of NAFTA, this average quadrupled to US$13.43 billion[22].

### 1. Direct foreign investment

This foreign investment was located in the most strategic and dynamic sectors in the Mexican economy. It was concentrated in the manufacturing sector (49.5 percent), which is the big exporter, in financial services (24.4 percent) and in commerce (10.8 percent). Three of the nine large sectors of the economy received 85.3 percent of the direct foreign investment during the NAFTA years. In contrast, in spite of the change in Mexico's constitution, there was virtually no foreign investment in the Mexican countryside, just 0.25 percent during the entire NAFTA period[23].

In addition, from a geographic perspective, the poorest areas were abandoned. Direct foreign investment during the

NAFTA period was highly concentrated in the most developed areas and nearly nonexistent in poorer areas and the country-side. The center of the country (the capital and the state of Mexico), and the northern or border zone (which, besides the maquiladora zone includes Monterrey, which is the other industrial center) received 90.15 percent of direct foreign investment. In contrast, the five poorest states received just 0.34 percent of that investment in spite of the fact that they also include developed areas and tourist zones such as Acapulco[24].

Once again, this is the result of leaving everything to the market. The poor areas and the agricultural sector will not receive large amounts of foreign investment if there is no deliberate policy by the state with government investments in infrastructure and probably other incentives. NAFTA, for its part, went in the opposite direction: deregulate and leave the destination of investment to pure market forces and profit maximization. Moreover, NAFTA limits the possibilities for an active policy on economic issues, since that would violate the commitments made on competition policy.

Certainly, private investment will not take place if there is no expectation of profits. It would be unreasonable to expect otherwise. It is for just that reason that public investment should create the conditions to attract it, but to attract it within a sustainable development plan agreed on by the communities involved.

Recently, an ambitious plan to attract foreign as well as national investment to a broad area of highly marginalized zones was proposed. That is, the Plan Puebla Panama. An explicit public policy to attract investment to such a depressed zone with such extreme poverty would be welcomed. However, when people saw the actual content of that plan, enthusiasm became disappointment and concern. Some of the main elements of Plan Puebla Panama and their foreseeable consequences are:

1   A broad bio-prospecting project that is designed to facilitate research and eventually patents on the zone's great

biodiversity by large corporations. They hope to patent the ancestral heritage of these indigenous zones. Where is the benefit for these marginalized communities?

2   A broad maquiladora corridor. Jobs would be welcome in this area, if they are good jobs with guarantees and labor rights, which are not characteristic in the maquiladoras. In reality, foreign investment will come to take advantage of labor that is even cheaper than at the border.

3   Large infrastructure and communications investments, but everything indicates that these will be projects planned by U.S. geo-strategic interests to compensate for the obsolescence of the Panama Canal, not investments decided on according Mexico's needs or those of the people living in those areas.

4   Broad zones for eucalyptus and palm oil plantations that would cause serious degradation of agricultural soil.

These investments do not appear to have been made with a view to the region's needs. Above all, there is no real incorporation of communities, who are mainly indigenous, in decisionmaking or in the design of the development projects. Indigenous communities fight for their autonomy precisely in order to define the sustainable use of their natural resources and the definition of their development. They fight to be subjects of law precisely in order to avoid being objects of development projects for others in their territory. This is what was denied to them with the changes in the constitutional reforms on indigenous rights and culture. In other words, investment is welcome, even foreign investment, in these depressed areas, but indigenous communities should be subjects of rights and not "objects" of plans defined elsewhere.

Beyond these characteristics of foreign investment, we find again the same paradox as in foreign trade. In spite of such large volumes of investment during these years, the economy has hardly grown at all. The reason is that in large part this investment has been used to buy existing companies[25], with another important portion invested in maquiladoras that are disconnected from national productive chains and thus have little effect on the economy as a whole. Nearly all banks have been sold; only one of the small banks is still not majority owned by foreigners. Nearly all of the large commercial chains have been sold, leaving a few of regional importance and one national chain that is currently in crisis. They have been associated in differing proportions with Mexican export industries that are also increasingly disconnected from national productive chains.

Direct foreign investment in underdeveloped countries is necessary, we do not have the luxury of rejecting it, but under the current rules it has few positive effects on the economy as a whole and it has resulted in the de-nationalization of much of our productive structure. We will return to this point later in the paper, but first we will examine the behavior of portfolio investment.

## 2. Portfolio Investment

Portfolio investment is investment in instruments, as opposed to direct investment, which is a physical investment such as building or buying a business, which in most cases implies controlling it. Portfolio investment is made using two kinds of instruments: 1) the purchase of stock in a company without that implying control over it; 2) purchase of debt bonds or debentures that can be public or private. The latter case is really debt contracted by those issuing the bonds, but in national accounting it is counted as foreign investment.

Foreign portfolio investment, and in particular investment in bonds[26] has been very unstable. Figure 1-1 shows the accumulated balances, as well as the many times of net dis-investment.

**Figure 1-1**
**Portfolio Investment: Bonds/Stocks: Accumulated Totals**

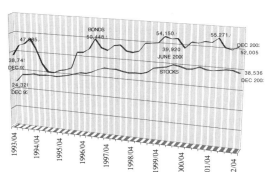

Source: Banco de México: Balance of Payments

Although the proportion of portfolio investment has decreased due the growth in direct investment, the accumulated total is quite large, US$90.54 billion, which indicates the country's enormous vulnerability should that investment suddenly leave.

Bonds are particularly volatile, since that investment can enter and leave the country on a whim, creating great vulnerability for the country. It is really debt, and very short-term debt. The accumulated total of debt bonds is even greater than before the 1994 crisis and, as in that time, is denominated in foreign currency. The economy thus remains vulnerable to a speculative run. Nothing has been learned from the successive crises. First there was the Mexican peso crisis and its "tequila" effect, then the Russian crisis, the Asian crisis, the Brazilian, and now the Argentine crisis[27]. The risks and consequences of the volatility of these investments are aggravated due to a "clean float" monetary policy. The state does not intervene in the exchange rate, not even through market mechanisms (buying and selling dollars). It could do so but it has decided not to. This means that our currency's stability is left completely to supply and demand,

and a large part of the supply depends on the permanence of these hot or speculative investments.

Direct foreign investment is favored by the privileges and rights granted to those investors under NAFTA. In contrast, there is nothing in NAFTA that favors the permanence or stability of portfolio investment. To the contrary, NAFTA guarantees absolute freedom for the circulation of capital.

There are no specific state policies to avoid the instability and vulnerability generated by this kind of hot investment either. In fact, the government even promotes it, offering high yields. In 1996, when the Mexican economy was being stabilized, portfolio investment once again predominated (it was 59 percent of all investment in the country that year). The same thing happened in 1999, when portfolio investment was 48 percent of the total. The governing elite did not learn the lesson of the past; the government once again issued papers denominated in foreign currency (US$9.71 billion). This was much worse than in 1993, before the crisis, when it was just 33 percent (US$10.8 billion).

In addition, policies were maintained that favored speculation. Profits from stock sales are not taxed. The fiscal reform presented by President Fox fails to record those profits in spite of the scandal caused by the sale of Banamex, the biggest Mexican bank. That bank was sold to Citibank for US$12.5 billion, and the stockholders did not pay even one peso in taxes on the profits generated by that sale. The scandal is even greater because the value of that bank includes the money injected by the government to bail it out after the 1994-1995 crisis, a debt that continues to be paid by our taxes.

During the NAFTA period there have been several periods of enormous capital flight. As can be seen in the following graph, this flight did not only happen during the 1995 crisis (US$16.95 billion left the country between September 1994 and September 1995). US$5.4 billion left the country between June and December 1997; US$3.2 billion left the country between June and December 1998. Portfolio investment dropped US$5.44 billion between March and December 2000, and US$3.71 billion left between March and December 2002.

### 3. Impacts and the terms of NAFTA

Direct investment has increased, which is good, but it is not well integrated into Mexico's national productive chains and therefore has not produced multiplier effects in terms of growth and employment. Nor has it contributed to narrowing the gap between marginalized areas and those that enjoy greater generation of wealth. Instead, it has reinforced this enormous regional disparity.

The amount of very short-term speculative, foreign-currency denominated speculative investment continues at high levels, and therefore keeps the Mexican economy in a state of high vulnerability to capital flight. The stability of the currency is completely subject to market forces, and therefore depends on that flight capital not leaving, and NAFTA makes nearly any kind of state intervention in that flight impossible.

None of these issues is unrelated to the terms under which NAFTA was negotiated[28]. In reality the treaty between the United States and Canada left the dynamics of foreign investment solely to market forces. It reduces, if not eliminates, the ability of the state to regulate it. It does not require national content as an element of the rules of origin. It prohibits nearly all performance requirements. Under these conditions, it is difficult to orient investment and make it play a positive role in national development. Foreign investors settle disputes not in the host country's court system according to national laws, but instead in supranational mechanisms[29]. In the framework of NAFTA, investors guarantee their rights with international legislation and leave the rights of their workers and the general population in the national sphere. Neither are environmental rights ensured against the profits of those investors.

Foreign trade and investment, instead of generating national development, have been consolidating enclaves or modern and highly competitive and profitable "islands" that are increasingly disconnected from the rest of the economy.

## III. Objective not achieved: growth

The average annual growth in GDP per capita during the nine years that NAFTA has been in place is just 0.96 percent. Accelerated, stable and sustainable growth had been sought and promised, but Mexico barely managed to grow. During this period there was a profound recession (1995) and another moderate recession (2001-2002). During the broadest period of implementation of the neoliberal model (1982-2002), the average rate of growth in GDP per capita is just 0.26 percent a year. People speak of the 1980s as the lost decade, but really there are twenty lost years in terms of generation of wealth. The accumulated balance of GDP per capita from 1982 to 2002 is just 5.6 percent[30]

The growth in exports and the attraction of foreign investment were the means for growth. The tools were achieved but not the objective. In reality, the neoliberal economic strategy, and within it NAFTA have resulted in the lowest rate of economic growth compared with any other economic strategy carried out by the country during the twentieth century, as can be seen in the graph below.

The explanation of this paradox that an economy with sales abroad of more than a trillion dollars and with inflows of more than US$150 billion has already been given. Exports were excessively concentrated and disconnected from the rest of the economy. They generated some successful enclaves, but their success did not spur on the rest of the economy, and much of the foreign investment was for the purchase of existing companies.

**Figure 1-2**
**Average Growth in GDP Per Capita**

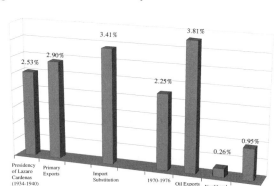

What is most dramatic is that this poor growth has also resulted in enormous environmental degradation. It is not only not sustainable, but predatory of nature and the environment. On average, the annual cost of environmental degradation and exhaustion is equivalent to 10 percent of GDP[31].

# IV. Employment

### 1. Some methodological notes

a)   A common question during discussions of NAFTA is if it really possible to isolate the direct effects of that accord. This is in part a false debate. We can recognize that it is not possible to isolate the Mexican statistics on employment or unemployment that is directly and absolutely related to NAFTA. But that is not as relevant as it seems. We have already said that NAFTA is nothing more than a law to stabilize a policy, an orientation, an economic strategy. Why is there such urgency to isolate what is due to NAFTA from what is the result of domestic economic policy? This is not to say that there are not specific and independent factors in

NAFTA that influence employment, they should be made explicit and not blamed on NAFTA. We will attempt to demonstrate the data most directly related to NAFTA and therefore give special relevance to the manufacturing sector that is responsible, as stated previously, for the vast majority of exports, as well as being the sector that receives half of all direct foreign investment.

Of course, the problem of unemployment and precarious employment is chronic in Mexico. This was the case long before NAFTA or even neoliberalism. Therefore the relevant methodological question is if the rules in NAFTA helped to reduce or, to the contrary, worsen the problem.

b) It is important to consider the balance of employment generation. Not just how many jobs were created in which sector or segment of the economy, but also how many were lost. This is important since the official Mexican propaganda speaks of many jobs being created in the export sector in order to demonstrate the wonders of NAFTA, but omits discussion of the jobs that were lost in the firms that used to provide inputs to those exporters, who in the past were Mexicans and now come from foreign suppliers. We will speak of jobs in the manufacturing sector as a whole.

c) Lastly, a word on Mexican statistical sources. General information on employment in Mexico is mainly offered in three sources that cover different sets of workers. The first is the national survey of urban employment, which only covers cities with over 100,000 inhabitants, which means it leaves out nearly half of the economically active population. There is also the Mexican Social Security Institute (IMSS), which covers only so-called formal employment. These two sources offer information every month, but they do not cover all workers. The only source of information with general geographic coverage and that includes both so-called formal and informal employment, urban as well as rural, is the National Employment Survey. We will favor the latter source due to its national coverage and the complete set of workers, which, starting in 2003, is published on a quarterly basis. On the other hand, there is some information on specific sectors. The manufacturing sector is particularly important. However, on the issue of employment, this survey has a distortion, recognized by National Geographic and Information Institute, in the sense that the sample favors large and medium-scale industry. In reality the sample is designed to achieve representation of the GDP for each one of the manufacturing sectors using the least possible number of surveys, but that implies favoring large companies, and therefore distorts information on employment. There is no other source of information, so with those reservations, we will use it.

### 2. Promises and myths

The NAFTA negotiators and promoters promised more and better jobs. This was one of the most repeated promises.

They now speak of thousands of jobs generated by the export sector. There is no doubt that large exporters and the maquiladoras have generated jobs; but, as stated previously, jobs were also lost by the former suppliers to those exporters.

### 3. The hard data of reality

There have not been either more or better jobs during the NAFTA period.

a) During the first nine years of NAFTA just 8,073,201 new jobs were created in the country; but that is a 46.6 percent deficit compared to the number necessary to provide jobs to people aged 15-64 entering the workforce[32].

b) In addition, these few jobs are bad jobs. Some 55.3 percent of new jobs do not provide any of the benefits required by law: social security; Christmas bonus; and ten days of vacation a year[33]. If we consider only formal wage-workers, 49.5 percent do not receive benefits[34].

c) So-called formal employment can be arrived at adding the data from the Mexican Social Security Institute (IMSS) and the Social Security Institute at the Service of State Workers (ISSSTE). During the NAFTA period, registration of workers in the social security system increased to 4,809,222, just 36 percent of workers.[35]

This is general data and of course these results are influenced by many factors, not just NAFTA. However, it does demonstrate the economic strategy's – of which NAFTA is a key element — poor capacity to generate growth and employment. Looking at more specific data linked to sectors that have benefited from NAFTA, we see:

d) The manufacturing sector accounted for 87.35 percent of the country's total exports during the NAFTA period[36] and 49.5 percent of total direct foreign investment[37]. It is a successful sector: it grew 37.95 percent during NAFTA, in spite of three years of recession or stagnation. However, there are now 9.4 percent (81,418) few jobs in that sector than before NAFTA[38]. In fact, jobs were created in the final export sector, but fewer than were lost in the former suppliers chain, since the export sector now imports nearly all of its inputs.

One might think that this is due to the stagnation-recession in the United States and Mexico in 2001 and 2002, but that is only part of the problem. The results of a strategy can not be judged only in the good years, and but over the medium term. The fact is that with three years of rapid growth and three years of recession, the sector grew nearly 40 percent and in terms of employment it lost nearly 10 percent. Moreover, leaving aside the last two years in which manufacturing declined, that is the year 2000, employment is nearly the same as it was seven years earlier (a loss of 0.2 percent). Jobs were lost during the deep recession in 1995 and the moderate recession in 2001 and 2002, but there was accelerated growth during the other years and in spite of this, there is a net loss of jobs.

One might think that few jobs were generated due to the fact that productivity was rising. In fact, that is part of the explanation; productivity increased 53.6 percent in the non-maquiladora manufacturing sector during the nine years of NAFTA[39]. In the maquiladora export sector it dropped 5.2 percent[40]. More is being produced with less labor, but his is only one factor in the explanation. Another factor is the export sectors' growing loss of connection to national production chains. Job creation in the big exporters does not translate into indirect job creation in the Mexican suppliers but instead in the foreign suppliers, which is to say it is a growth plan in which indirect jobs are created abroad.

It is not that we oppose progress and improvements in efficiency. It is good that productivity increases as long as the benefits are distributed so that workers benefit. The fact is that during the nine years of NAFTA the price of labor (including wages, benefits and indirect costs such as what the employer pays for social security) have fallen in real terms by 36 percent. So workers are producing 53 percent more per hour of work and it costs the employers 36 percent less for this productive work.

In summary, this is a sector that in spite of some bad years has grown significantly, but has lost rather than generated jobs because there are fewer jobs created than are lost due to the loss of old national suppliers. It is good that the sector is modernizing and becoming more competitive (productivity) but very bad that this has not benefited but instead has hurt workers (fewer jobs and reduction in their incomes).

e) Within the manufacturing sector it is assumed that the maquiladora sector is the big job generator. The maquiladora export industry is responsible for nearly half of the country's total exports (45.18 percent) and receives 15.8 percent of direct foreign investment. However, on average, since NAFTA began the maquiladoras have created 59,814 jobs[41] and we should remember that the country needs 1,400,000 jobs per year. Regionally, in some municipalities with a large maquiladora presence, it does serve to mitigate unemployment, but not at the national level.

## Conclusion

NAFTA has not fulfilled the expectations and objectives proposed by its promoters.

It has not even achieved significant economic growth, at least not stable, sustained and sustainable growth with social justice.

The low growth rate has been at the cost of enormous environmental degradation and natural resource depletion.

It has not created more and better jobs.

To the contrary, it has accelerated the disintegration of national production chains.

It has also accelerated the denationalization of our national productive structure. There are now nearly no Mexican banks or commercial chains, and most large export companies are majority owned by foreigners (with very few exceptions).

The strategy did not work because of the rules and modalities governing our insertion into the global economy. Exports have not been the engine for the economy as a whole due to their disconnection from national productive linkages. Much is exported, but those exports are highly concentrated in a few companies and they are like islands or enclaves with very few spin-offs on local production chains and in the creation of indirect employment. There has been a great deal of direct foreign investment, but it has also failed to contribute significantly to growth and job creation since much of it is the purchase of existing companies.

There are few winners and many losers. NAFTA has generated a few islands of economic success, very successful in terms of profits for their owners, but the economy as a whole has not benefited.

Taking stock of this situation should lead to a rethinking of the way Mexico has integrated into the global economy. NAFTA is not a model that other countries should imitate. We can not leave our countries' future solely to market forces. A viable national development plan is necessary, and a struggle for international rules and regulations that create the conditions for each country to optimize its potential for development. We do not need more free-trade agreements, that is, deregulation and holding competition above all else, in a situation in which the big fish eats the little fish. We need international agreements for sustainable development and income distribution at both the global level and within each country. Another world is possible, another globalization is possible and there are advanced proposals toward that end.

# Chapter 2
# NAFTA's Impact on Mexican Agriculture: An Overview

by Manuel Ángel Gómez Cruz[42] and Rita Schwentesius Rindermann[43]

## Introduction

The purpose of this text is to document and describe the economic and social impacts of *North American Free Trade Agreement's (NAFTA) Agriculture Chapter*, both in the present and for the future, with the aim of justifying through objective data the urgent need to review that chapter of the trade agreement in order to establish protection mechanisms for some agricultural products.

It could be argued that in late 1993, when the National Congress gave its approval for the Executive Branch to sign the trade agreement, the implications were not known, the decision was not reached democratically, and the optimism felt by producers was unfounded. Today, in the year 2003, the situation is completely different, since we have witnessed NAFTA's disastrous impacts on Mexico's agricultural sector.

This document is composed essentially of four parts:
1 Background
2 Asymmetries
3 A ten-year evaluation of NAFTA
4 Proposals

## I. Background: Studies conducted from 1991 to the present

Research studies conducted by organizations of small, medium and large producers and by different academic groups

(Universidad Autónoma Nacional de México, Universidad Autónoma Metropolitana, El Colegio de México, the United States and Canada, in coordination with the Center for Economic, Social, and Technology Research on World Agriculture and Agribusiness (CIESTAAM) of Autonomous University of Chapingo (UACh) of Mexico during the period since 1991, have by and large reached the following conclusions: *In general, Mexico has little to gain and much to lose from the trade agreement with the United States and Canada, and therefore [CIESTAAM] recommended against negotiating from positions that jeopardize the domestic production of our most important foods — primarily grains, dairy products and meat— in order to avoid severe damage to the national industry and to avoid an unacceptable intensification of dependency in terms of food and in economic, technological and even political terms.*[44] Based on the readily observed consequences, a partial suspension of NAFTA (Chapter VII on Agriculture) has been advocated since 2000.

In the year 2002, the World Bank came to similar conclusions: "It can be said that [the rural] sector has been the object of the most drastic structural reforms (trade liberalization as promoted by GATT and NAFTA, elimination of price controls, structural reform in relation to land ownership), however the results have been *disappointing* (authors' emphasis): stagnation of growth, lack of competitiveness in the international market, an increase in poverty in rural areas…. This sets forth a significant political problem, since beginning in 2008, NAFTA will place this sector in open competition with Canada and the United States."[45]

Since the end of 2002, Mexican farmers, who are organized in a wide variety of ways, have been clear about the situation they face and have been insisting that *The rural sector can't take any more (El campo no aguanta más).* A struggle began not only against the government and against transnational corporations, but also against Mexico's long-standing corporative-style farmer organizations. There was a protest march involving more than 100,000 persons on January 31, 2003 which culminated at Mexico City's central plaza. The fact that this event was tolerated and accepted by the citizens of that enormous city (although usually, marches of this type provoke a great deal of irritation) is an indicator of the solidarity and sympathy for the farmers engaged in this current struggle. It also demonstrates that the farmer movement has not died and has the capacity to renovate itself.

## II. Importance of agriculture

In Mexico there are at least two completely opposite positions on the agricultural sector's importance in the economy and NAFTA's impact. The first position measures the importance of this sector solely in monetary terms, based on its contribution to the GDP, and it evaluates NAFTA's impact exclusively through trade statistics.

The other position (presented here) considers the following: a) the multiplier effect of the agricultural sector, in both vertical and horizontal directions, or in other words, it measures the impact on the manufacturing and inputs industries, and on the transportation, services and trade sectors; and b) the multifunctionality (multi-functional nature) of this sector, as the foundation for food and food sovereignty, as a creator of jobs and foreign currency, and considering its impact on society, and its importance in maintaining peace in rural areas, for protecting the environment, biodiversity and the landscape, as the basis for our culture in terms of the food we eat, and an important part of our national identity, etc. This second position acknowledges the existence of a number of different rural sectors in Mexico, leading to the necessity for differentiated policies toward the types of producers and regions characterizing our country.

Nevertheless, the first position is the one that prevails in Mexico's current policies (Realpolitik), and all the tendencies organized around the second perception are scorned and suppressed. Measures are implemented to provide assistance[46] and protection[47] only for large agricultural producers and for groups associated with U.S. capital, while agricultural policy is reduced to a type of charity that leads nowhere.

## III. Asymmetries

Trade relations between Mexico and its trading partners, the United States and Canada, are characterized by numerous asymmetries that explain, to a significant degree, NAFTA's negative impact on the agricultural sector:

Since before the signing of NAFTA:

- Asymmetries in natural resources, levels of technology, producers' capitalization, assistance and subsidies received, etc. (see Table 1A in the Annex).

- Noncompetitive production costs in Mexico, due to higher prices for inputs such as diesel and electricity, and financial costs; and higher costs in marketing products (due to deficient, poor-quality infrastructure in highways and warehouse storage, lack of information, etc.). These are costs over which producers have no influence.

- NAFTA was poorly negotiated for Mexico: a) the agreement was negotiated without considering the complete experience of Free Trade Agreement between the United States and Canada; also, chapters 19 and 20, referring to trade-related disputes and controversies, establish inadequate processes for genuinely resolving conflicts, and their contents lead to a vicious circle that holds no solutions; b) the most sensitive products were not excluded, as they were for Canada (poultry products, milk products); high import quotas without tariffs were accepted for a broad range of products; there is no provision for the possibility of review, suspension, moratorium or the use of other instruments for protecting national production.

- Unequal legal status: the United States negotiated a Free Trade Agreement, while in the case of Mexico it is acknowledged as a Treaty, which therefore has different legal implications, including limitations on reviewing NAFTA.
- The United States has greater negotiating capability and power (it makes use of lobbying, ongoing evaluation studies, etc.).

After the signing of the Agreement:
- With the new US Farm Bill 2002,[48] farmers in that country receive 70% more assistance. In Mexico subsidies represent 19% of farm income, while in the United States, subsidies account for 21%.[49]
- The methodology used by the OECD (Organization for Economic Cooperation and Development) for estimating assistance to farmers indicates a major inconsistency in agricultural assistance in Mexico. Before NAFTA, the levels of assistance in the United States and Canada were already much greater than in Mexico, and since NAFTA, 33% of the value of agricultural production in the United States has been subsidized, and in Mexico, only 16%.[50, 51]

**Figure 2-1.**
**Agriculture Support Estimates for Mexico, United States and Canada, 1986-2001 (% of the value of agricultural production)**

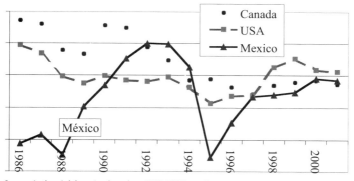

Source: Authors' elaboration based on: OECD, 2002, *op. cit.*

- Also, U.S. farmers receive assistance in the amount of US $120.00 per hectare,[52] while in Mexico, this amount is equivalent to only US $45.00 (OECD). U.S. producers farm an average of 29 hectares (arable land), while Mexican farmers cultivate only 1.8 hectares (FAO, Statistical Database). Finally, the productivity of a U.S. agricultural worker is 18 times greater (US $39,000) when compared to a worker in Mexico (US $2,164), according to data from the World Bank.

- There are asymmetries in relation to the use of the limitations negotiated in NAFTA. In practice, Mexico has not made use of the limitations it negotiated: it has never charged tariffs on imports beyond the negotiated quotas for corn and beans, and consequently, in the case of corn, the fiscal loss during the NAFTA period has been nearly US $2.9 billion (see Table 2-1), and in the case of beans, US $77 million, from imports originating from the United States alone.[53]

- Mexico has not made sufficient progress in defining standards, which has resulted in the entry of tariff-free imports,

## Table 2-1
## Mexico. Fiscal Loss in the Case of Corn Imports, 1994-2001

| Año | Import (ton) | Quota (ton) | Overquota (ton) | Tariff (NAFTA) (US $/ton) | Fiscal loss (US$) |
|---|---|---|---|---|---|
| 1989-1993 | 2,148,215 | | | | |
| 1994 | 3,054,111 | 2,575,000 | 479,111 | 197 | 94,384,867 |
| 1995 | 5,945,500 | 2,652,250 | 3,293,350 | 189 | 622,424,250 |
| 1996 | 6,348,561 | 2,731,817 | 3,616,744 | 181 | 654,630,664 |
| 1997 | 2,594,580 | 2,813,771 | 0 | 173 | 0 |
| 1998 | 5,277,342 | 2,898,184 | 2,379,158 | 164 | 390,181,912 |
| 1999 | 5,096,207 | 2,985,129 | 2,111,078 | 156 | 329,328,168 |
| 2000 | 5,179,134 | 3,074,682 | 2,104,452 | 139 | 292,518,828 |
| 2001 | 5,654,721 | 3,166,922 | 2,487,799 | 121 | 301,023,679 |
| 2002 | 5,337,124 | 3.261,930 | 2,075,194 | 104 | 215,820,176 |
| 2003 | | 3,359,788 | | 87 | |
| 2004 | | 3,460,581 | | 69 | |
| 2005 | | 3,564,399 | | 52 | |
| 2006 | | 3,671,331 | | 34 | |
| 2007 | | 3,781,470 | | 17 | |
| 2008 | | **Free** | | 0 | |
| **TOTAL** | **45,798,371** | | | | **2,900,312,544** |

Source: Authors' calculations based on: USDA, ERS, Foreign Agricultural Trade of the United States (http://www.fas.usda.gov/ustrdscripts/USReport.exe) y SECOFI, 1994, *Tratado de Libre Comercio de América del Norte. Fracciones arancelarias y plazos de desgravación. México*: Miguel Ángel Porrúa, Librero Editor, pp. 78-80.

and the lack of plant and animal sanitation controls, for example in the case of meat products.

- Mexico has not implemented serious measures to confront the existence of contraband activity, e.g., in the cases of beans and rice.

## IV. A ten-year evaluation

After ten years, the impact from NAFTA is more dramatic than predicted:

- The public budget for Mexico's agriculture and fisheries sectors was reduced in real terms on a continuous basis throughout the 1990 to 2002 period. The amount decreased from 75,998 million pesos in 1994, the year NAFTA began, to less than 50% of that amount by the year 2001 (see Figure 2-2).

- Mexico's overall agro-food sector is not competitive in the NAFTA region (see Figure 2-3). Although it was previously competitive in the 1960s, it has gradually lost ground to the extent that it is currently unable to narrow the gap with respect to the United States.

**Figure 2-2**
**Mexico. Government budget for rural development, 1990-2001 (mill. of 2001 pesos)**

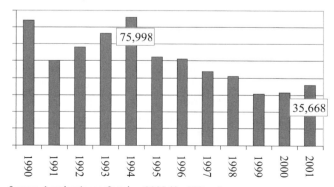

Source: Agrobusiness, October 2002, No. 119, p. 1.

**Figure 2-3**
**Competitiveness of Mexican and US agro-food sectors, 1961-2001**

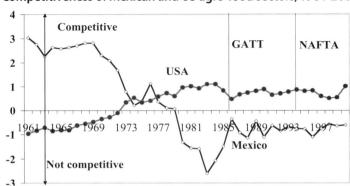

Source: Authors' calculations based on Index of Vollrath,[56] based on dates from
FAO, http:// apps.fao.org

- In 1993, before NAFTA, Mexico imported 8.8 million metric tons of grains and oilseeds, however for the year 2002 it is estimated that Mexico will have imported more than 20 million metric tons, or 2.3 times more. Since NAFTA, 136.6 million metric tons have been imported. A similar situation can be found with regard to meat, tropical fruits, etc. These imports have replaced national products, increasing rural unemployment and furthermore, part of the country's physical infrastructure has been destroyed.

- Mexico has a chronic agricultural trade deficit, with an increasing tendency. Nine years since NAFTA went into effect, the deficit has reached a level of US $14.5 billion. This amount is equivalent to 4.3 times the proposed 2003 budget for agriculture (see Figure 2-4).

- Statistics indicate that Mexico is losing its food sovereignty, and instead has a greater dependency on imports, generating a major loss in foreign currency. In grains and oilseeds alone, Mexico imported US $30 billion between 1994 and September 2002,[54] and every year, its food dependency increases (see Figure 2-5). Since NAFTA, Mexico has spent the exorbitant amount of US $78 billion to purchase food,

## Figure 2-4
## Mexico. Food Imports and trade balance, 1989-2002 (millions of US$)

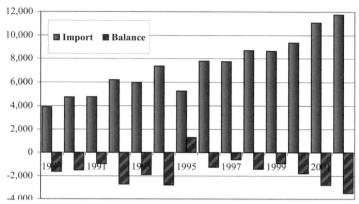

Source: INEGI, http://www.inegi.gob.mx

## Figure 2-5
## Mexico. Tendency of decreasing grain self-sufficiency, 1961-2000 (% of consumption)

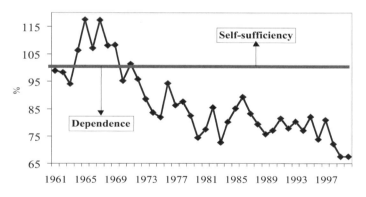

Source: Authors' calculations based on: FAO, http://apps.fao.org

an amount greater than the country's foreign debt (US $73,658,600).[55]

- Unemployment in rural Mexico is increasing at an alarming rate. According to data from the Department of Labor and Social Security, 1.78 million jobs have been lost,[57] and of that amount, nearly 600,000 are related to basic grain production. Some 40% of pork producers have stopped producing, and 24% of potato producers have done the same, with similar results in the cases of rice and corn producers, among others.

- Poverty has increased despite NAFTA —which was supposed to attract more foreign investment in agriculture, as well as generate more jobs and increase worker remunerations. According to official statistics, 69.3% of the total rural population is poor.[58]

- The supposed advantages for consumers based on greater access to less expensive, imported food products turned out to be pure rhetoric. From 1994 to 2002, the prices in the basic food basket have increased 257%, while prices paid

**Figure 2-6**
**Mexico. Indices of prices in the basic food basket, prices paid to agricultural producers and minimum wages, 1994-2002 (1994=100)**

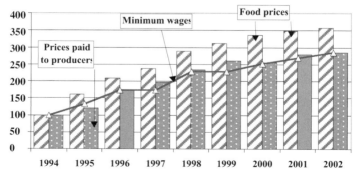

Sources: Authors' calculations based on: Presidencia de la República, 2° Informe de Gobierno, 2 de septiembre de 2002. Anexo, p. 210 y 309.

to agricultural producers rose only 185%, according to statistics from the Mexican government (see Figure 2-6). In other words, massive imports have increased pressure on prices for primary agricultural producers, and have not lowered prices for consumers, and in fact, the latter have continued to increase.

- Finally, NAFTA has caused the most profound, drastic transformation in the history of Mexican agriculture. The present and future for this sector has been totally changed. The option of continuing to live in rural areas has been placed in doubt for the great majority of the thousands of Mexican farmers. Organizations of small, medium and business-level producers of corn, soybeans, wheat, beans, rice, potatoes, cotton, apples, pork, cattle, etc. —representing the great majority of the country's farmers— are calling for the suspension of NAFTA, or at least its renegotiation, because those who have come out ahead with NAFTA are no more than a thousand individuals,[59] while millions are on the losing end.

- Mexico's Executive Branch does not listen; it does not see or hear. It says everything is fine in rural Mexico, and opposition to NAFTA is nothing more than sensationalism.[60] The same discourse is repeated by government officials in the Departments of Economy and Agriculture and the Foreign Ministry.

## V. Prospects for 2003

- As of January 1, 2003, nine years after NAFTA's implementation, the remaining minimal tariff protection for all imported agricultural products was eliminated, with the exception of corn, beans, powdered milk and sugar, although the protections for these latter products is only on paper.

- Among the products that will suffer the most during 2003 are the following:
  - Poultry
  - Pork
  - Potatoes
  - Animal fats
  - Barley
  - Apples
  - Fresh cheeses
  - These sectors will still have tariff protection ranging from 25 to 50% and/or import quotas until December 31. We can expect that beginning on January 1, importers will take advantage of the new circumstances.
- Also as of January 2003, poultry and pork meat production is no longer protected through import quotas. According to well-informed sources in the Mexican government, we know that in recent years importers of poultry and pork asked to import up to ten times the tariff-free quota negotiated in NAFTA. A dramatic increase in imports of these products is expected, which will not only negatively impact Mexico's poultry and pork sectors but also the beef-producing sector. Already in the fall of 2002 many cattle ranchers in the states of Tabasco and Veracruz were liquidating their herds and no longer investing in this activity. Meat imports also negatively impact the production of animal feed, for which there is a constantly decreasing national demand.
- Protection will also disappear for barley and malt production which could turn Mexico into a beer *maquila* country.
- In addition, there is an incredible list of primary products and processed goods that will be free from tariffs, including: rice; tropical fruits; wheat; edible by-products; even coffee! (roasted and processed); dairy products (except powdered milk); milled products; fresh grape wines; canned

and other processed goods; tobacco; vegetable oil and fats; copra, and sheep (meat and live animals).

- In addition, the United States will make it even more difficult for Mexican products to be introduced in that country. Some examples can be seen in the new study on alleged dumping by Mexican tomato exporters and the prohibition of cantaloupe entering the United States, supposedly due to sanitation problems, which as of the end of November 2002 has not been duly demonstrated.

## VI. Proposal

An important precedent can be seen in the role of the U.S. Congress in the case of transportation. Despite the fact that NAFTA established the unrestricted movement of vehicles between Mexican and U.S. territories beginning in 1995, our neighboring government used a moratorium to prohibit Mexican vehicles from entering the United States. After many years of controversy, on February 6, 2001, the WTO issued a decision in favor of Mexico. On June 5, 2001 President Bush finally gave authorization (on paper) for Mexican trucks to enter the United States and ordered the lifting of the 1995 moratorium. However, the U.S. Congress approved U.S. access for Mexican cargo trucks to begin in the year 2002, with the condition that sufficient inspectors could be contracted. On August 1, 2001, however, it violated the agreement, calling for a blockade, using the justification of the lack of safety represented by Mexican trucks on U.S. highways.[61] Thus, the U.S. Congress is showing us the way. Despite NAFTA, they protect their transportation sector, their sources of employment and their nationalist interests.

Given the strategic role played by agriculture as a source of employment, a producer of food, important in the protection of the environment, with social and cultural implications, and given that there are no compensation funds to lessen the effects of NAFTA, and the fact that whatever budget is designated will never be enough to allow Mexico's agricultural sector to be competitive with the agricultural sector in the world's most powerful country, and in consideration of Article 21 of the WTO (on the consequences of a Treaty) and Article 89 of the Constitution, Section 10 (unequal legal status, see Annex), and given the faculties granted by the nation to the legislative branch, it is proposed that the NAFTA agriculture chapter be reviewed. Mexico should not give up its national sovereignty and should take advantage of all the provisions stipulated in its Constitution.

This proposal is not only justified by the damages already caused by NAFTA, but also due to the threat of what is to come, beginning in 2003.

A review and the partial suspension of NAFTA to protect the country's most sensitive products will affect some individual interests, especially those of importers and intermediaries for agricultural products. However, as we have demonstrated, the benefits for consumers have not appeared. And, Mexican exporters will not feel any negative effects as long as they make use of the *maneuvering spaces* permitted by the WTO *for developing countries*.

It is also important to take into consideration the direct and indirect monetary expenditures that Mexican society has already paid for trade liberalization, as well as those still to come. The liquidation of BANRURAL alone will cost the overall Mexican society 42 billion pesos (an amount that surpasses the agricultural budget for the entire year 2002). BANRURAL 's failure cannot be explained solely due to administrative errors, but rather due to the lack of profitability in agriculture as a result of the State policy of abandoning its responsibilities.

Finally, the Mexican State implemented the policy of economic liberation and signed NAFTA —without democratically consulting the society— and now it must take responsibility for the damage caused and must implement policies that ben-

## Table 2-2
## Asymmetries between Mexico, United States and Canada

| | Mexico | United States | Canada |
|---|---|---|---|
| Population (1,000)[1] | 100,368 | 285,926 | 31,015 |
| Rural Population (1,000) [1] | 25,555 | 64,539 | 6,535 |
| Agricultural Population (1,000) [1] | 23,064 | 6,162 | 766 |
| Population density (people of sq. km)[2] | 51 | 30 | 3 |
| Surface area (1,000 ha)[2] | 195,820 | 962,909 | 997,061 |
| Arable land (1,000 ha)[2] | 27,300 | 179,000 | 45,700 |
| Irrigated land (1,000 ha)[3] | 6,500 | 22,400 | 720 |
| GNP US$ mil mill. (1999)[4] | 428.8 (place 12) | 8,351.0 (place 1) | 591.4 (place 9) |
| GNP per capita (US$ 1999) [4] | 4,400 (place 71) | 30,600 (place 8) | 19,320 (place 29) |
| GINI index[4] | 53.7 | 40.8 | 31.5 |
| Percentage share of income, highest 10% [4] | 42.8 | 30.5 | 23.8 |
| Competitiveness ranking, 2001[6] | 51 | 2 | 11 |
| Growth competitiveness ranking, 2001[6] | 42 | 2 | 3 |
| Public expenditure on agricultural research/ag. GNP (%) | 0.52 | 2.60 | |
| Public expenditure on education (% of GNP)[4] | 4.9 | 5.4 | 6.9 |
| Tractors per 1,000 agricultural workers [4] | 20 | 1,484 | 1,642 |
| Agricultural wages (US$ per year), 1995/98[5] | 908 | n.d. | 30,625 |
| Agricultural productivity (1995 US$ per agricultural worker) [4] | 2,164 | 39,001 | n.d. |
| Annual deforestation (annual % change)[4] | 0.9 | -0.3 * | -0.1* |
| Producer support estimates (% of value of production) 2001[7] | 22 | 36 | 25 |
| Food import, 1998/2000, value (1,000 US$)[8] | 8,935,732 | 43,354,622 | 11,046,062 |
| Food exports, 1998/2000, value (1,000 US$)[8] | 7,157,371 | 55,508,420 | 15,253,898 |
| Trade balance, value (1,000 US$)[8] | -1,778,361 | 12,153,798 | 4,207,837 |
| Corn yields (t/ha)[9] | 2.50 | 8.55 | 7.15 |

n.d., not defined, * negative value means deforestation.

Sources:

1) http://apps1.fao.org/servlet/XteServlet.jrun?Areas=33&Areas=231&Areas=138&Items=3008& Elements-
=511&Elements=551&Elements=571&Years=2001&Format=Table&Xaxis=Years&Yaxis= Countries&
Aggregate=&Calculate=&Domain=SUA&ItemTypes=Population&Language=espanol&UserName=

2) http://apps.fao.org/servlet/XteServlet.jrun?Areas=33&Areas=231&Areas=138&Items=1421&
Elements=11&Elements=121&Elements=61&Years=2000&Format=Table&Xaxis=Years&Yaxis=Countries&Aggregate=&Calculat
e=&Domain=LUI&ItemTypes=LandUse&Language=espanol&UserName=

3) FAO, http://apps1.fao.org/servlet/XteServlet.jrun?Areas=33&Areas=231&Areas=138&Items=1423&
Elements=51&Years=2000&Format=Table&Xaxis=Years&Yaxis=Countries&Aggregate=&Calculate=&Domain=LUI&Item
Types=Irrigation&Language=espanol&UserName=

4) Banco Mundial, World Development Report 2000/2001. Attacking Poverty. Washington, DC, 2001.

5) The World Bank, World development Indicators 2002. Washington, DC, 2002, pp. 64 y 65.

6) World Economic Forum. *The Global Competitiveness Report 2001-2002*, Table 1. Overall competitiveness ranking, p. 15,
http://www.weforum.org/pdf/gcr/Overall_Competitiveness_Rankings.pdf,

7) OECD, *Agricultural Compendium*, Producer and Consumer Support Estimates 2002, base de datos, Beyond 20/20 Browser Files.
París, Francia, 2002.

8) FAO, http://apps1.fao.org/servlet/XteServlet.jrun?Areas=33&Areas=231&Areas=138&Items=1882&Elements
=62&Elements=92&Years=2000&Years=1999&Years=1998&Format=Table&Xaxis=Years&Yaxis=Countries&Aggregate=&Calcul
ate=&Domain=SUA&ItemTypes=Trade.CropsLivestockProducts&Language=espanol&UserName=

9) http://apps1.fao.org/servlet/XteServlet.jrun?Areas=33&Areas=231&Areas=138&Items=56&Elements=
41&Years=2001&Years=2000&Years=1999&Format=Table&Xaxis=Years&Yaxis=Countries&Aggregate=&Calculate=&Domain=S
UA&ItemTypes=Production.Crops.Primary&Language=espanol&UserName=

efit the overall society. It cannot remove itself from the consequences of its policies and above all, it must be clear about its responsibility for the well-being of its population.

# Chapter 3
# NAFTA at 10: an Assessment
## by David Ranney, Alliance for Responsible Trade

When NAFTA was being debated more than a decade ago, its proponents argued that this so-called "free trade agreement" would create more jobs through increased exports and that these jobs would be of high quality in terms of wages and benefits. Economic growth generated by trade, it was argued, would promote economic equality and a reduction of poverty. Higher rates of productivity due to more efficient production under heightened competition would protect U.S. workers' standard of living. Special side agreements would protect the environment and labor rights. The premise of these claims is that a reduction of trade barriers and the removal of regulations and limitations on capital flows will improve the living standards of all who participate. "Free Trade will lift all boats," it is said. As a result, more deliberate industrial and employment policies geared to the creation, maintenance and training for high quality, living wage jobs has all but been abandoned.

Now, after 10 years, none of these claims have come to pass. In fact the exact opposite has been true. We do not claim here that NAFTA alone has caused all of the problems in the economy that we document below. But we believe it has made them worse. And more importantly NAFTA is now only one part – a very important part – of a global model of "free trade" that glorifies the workings of a deregulated market, demonizes government planning and regulation, and views human beings and civil society as little more than customers in a continental shopping mall. It is, in the words of Canadian activist, Maude Barlow a "corporate bill of rights." But these rights exclude ordinary people and their government representatives and often work to our detriment. During the past decade, proponents of

NAFTA have also pushed similar policies as part of World Bank and IMF Structural Adjustment programs, World Trade Organization (WTO) rules, various bi lateral and multi lateral agreements such as the recent trade agreement between the U.S. and Chile and the so called Africa Opportunity Act. They are presently pushing for a Free Trade Area of the Americas (FTAA) to include all of the nations of this hemisphere (except Cuba) and they are attempting to expand the scope of the World Trade Organization.

NAFTA is a critical part of all these policy initiatives. Canada and Mexico are the United States' number 1 and 2 trade partners respectively in terms of the volume of exports. Together they represent 39% of all U.S. trade activity. If we were to add the proposed FTAA nations to this mix the volume would expand to 46% of U.S. exports. The importance of Canada and Mexico and the other FTAA nations to the U.S. economy is even greater when we consider the volume of capital flows within the region.

For these reasons we need to look both specifically at impacts of trade and investment flows within the North America region on the U.S. but also whether after 10 years of NAFTA and other similar trade agreements around the world this model of trade and investment is living up to the promises its proponents have made to us. If their promises have not been kept, as we believe to be the case, it is high time we consider alternatives.

## I. NAFTA and Employment

During the debate over NAFTA in the early 1990s, the government claimed that increased exports would create thousands of new jobs. The Commerce Department continues to make that claim but uses a crude, unsubstantiated multiplier that asserts that $1 billion in exports is worth between 15,000 and 20,000 jobs. In the analysis that follows, we demonstrate that this is simply not true.

For one thing, these estimates don't consider the fact that workers lose jobs due to NAFTA and related "free trade" policies. The exact number of U.S. workers negatively affected by NAFTA is difficult to calculate. A special act of Congress created a program of benefits for workers who have been certified as having lost jobs due to NAFTA. As of July 30, 2002 the number stood at 413,123.[62] Most would agree that this figure grossly understates the number of job losses that were directly caused by NAFTA because many workers don't know about the program and others apply for relief under a more generic trade adjustment program. Also only workers who produce products can qualify. Service producers are not eligible. Also workers who lose jobs indirectly to NAFTA such as auto parts suppliers who close a business because the auto plant to which they supply parts moved to Mexico would not be eligible. Thus the number of jobs lost directly and indirectly to NAFTA is considerably higher than the 413,123 workers certified under the NAFTA Trade Adjustment Assistance program.

NAFTA supporters argue that the deal has created a large number of U.S. jobs, based on the increase in U.S. exports to Canada and Mexico. However, it is important to also assess the impact of increased imports from Mexico and Canada (the Economic Policy Institute has conducted extensive analysis of this impact). An excess of imports over exports (a negative balance of trade) is a problem for several reasons. One is that workers in the U.S. can and do lose their jobs due to import competition and when this is not offset by expanded exports the result is a net loss. Job losses due to rising import competition at minimum have generated considerable job instability. And, as we will see later in this report, this often means that many workers end up in jobs paying lower wages and benefits.

The fact is that the U.S. has been running increasingly negative trade balances as the U.S. has liberalized trade with other nations worldwide. And this is specifically the case with NAFTA. As of October 2002, the cumulative balance of trade was $–

382.4 billion (meaning that the value of imports from other nations was $382.4 billion more than the value of our exports. With respect to NAFTA, the balance with Canada and Mexico was $-73.1 billion. As noted earlier, Canada and Mexico account for 39% of all trade activity. It is important to note that prior to the passage of NAFTA, the U.S. had a trade surplus with Mexico. In 1993 we still had a surplus of over $1.7 billion. By 2000 that surplus had turned into an annual deficit of $25 billion. In the case of Canada an earlier Canada-U.S. free trade agreement has been in effect since 1989. By 1993 we had a trade deficit with Canada of $10.8 billion. And by 2000 that deficit stood at $44.9 billion due in part to the devaluation of the Canadian dollar (see Canada report). Other potential FTAA nations had a balance of $-14.7 billion. That raises the hemispheric balance (which accounts for 46% of all U.S. trade) to $-87.8 billion. Presumably the passage of the FTAA will inflate this negative balance even more.

Furthermore, five major industrial groups, which include the U.S.' most important export products, also have negative trade balances, negating much of the benefit for U.S. workers of increased exports due to trade liberalization. As of October 2002, these include chemicals ($-7.2 billion); plastics ($-2.6 billion); electrical machinery and equipment ($-15.8 billion); transportation equipment ($ -76.2 billion); and computers/electronic equipment ($-71.2 billion).

## II. NAFTA, "Free Trade" and Labor

During the NAFTA debate there was controversy over the impact of the agreement on worker rights. The Clinton Administration responded with a weak side agreement designed to gain some labor support. But that side agreement is so toothless and cumbersome that it has never effectively protected the rights of workers. Furthermore, as we feared, the greater ease of moving operations out of the U.S. has given management the ability to use the threat of moving to undermine job quality, suppressing wages and lowering unionization rates. When firms actually do move, jobs are lost. They are not lost because of the increased competition of imports, but due to availability of lower wages elsewhere.

A comprehensive study on the use of the threat of moving concludes that this has been a significant kind of impact of both NAFTA and the rise of capital mobility generally.[63] Kate Bronfenbrenner's studies reveal that the threat of plant closing or moving (especially to Mexico) has been a frequent tactic used by U.S. employers in bargaining with their workers over wages and working conditions and in thwarting union organizing drives. And this tactic is increasing in frequency over time. Between 1992 and 1995 over half of employers used the threat of closing and/or moving production during union organizing drives and the threats continued during negotiations after successful drives. By 1998 the threat to close during organizing drives was up to 62% and it increased to 68% by 1999. Furthermore, between 1998 and 1999 in 18% of the campaigns where such threats were used, the threat was specifically a move to Mexico.

It is difficult to determine specifically what the impact of such threats has been on worker wages and working conditions. But it is clear that the success rate of union organizing drives declined as the threats rose. The average annual number of new union members gained through organizing drives dropped from about 300,000 in the mid 1970s to less than 100,000 by the mid 1990s. And the combination of the actual movement of production activity out of unionized sectors and failed union organizing campaigns has resulted in a significant decline in union membership in the U.S. Between 1990 and 2000, the percentage of unionized wage and salaried workers in the U.S. dropped from 16 % to 13%. The percentage of private sector unionized workers is much lower, standing at about 9% in 2000. An indication of the impact of this on wages can be seen in the fact that in 1998 average union wages were $2.66 higher per hour than non-union wages and the union workers worked, on average, about a half hour more each week.

## III. Employment Growth, Distribution, Wages and Benefits

NAFTA supporters have claimed that growth generated by trade would not only generate employment but that the new jobs would be of higher quality due to the greater efficiency of this economic development model. Once again, this has simply not been the case.

One argument made by NAFTA proponents in this regard is that higher rates of productivity due to more efficient production and heightened competition will protect U.S. workers' standard of living. Productivity has increased during the decade, but wages relative to this productivity growth have lost considerable ground. While productivity increased by 25% between 1990 and 2000, real wage growth was only 8%. Thus in an era of high capital mobility and declining unionization rates, the relationship of wages to productivity has come apart. And the result has been lower living standards for workers.

U.S. employment did grow during the late 1990s. But in the context of mobile capital and growing trade deficits, that growth redistributed employment into industries that pay lower wages and offer fewer benefits. Broadly we can see the shift through the fact that between 1990 and 2000 manufacturing industries lost 1.5 million jobs. The percentage of manufacturing jobs relative to total employment fell from 18% in 1990 to less than 15% in 2000. Meanwhile service sector employment grew by 10.5 million jobs and retail and wholesale trade jobs increased by 3 million jobs. Service sector jobs accounted for 99% of net new jobs created during the 1990s.[64]

Furthermore, this broad measure of the shift does not begin to tell the whole story because the service sector includes a wide range of industries paying different wages. What is more telling is the fact that there has been a high rate of job displacement during the period and that such displacement has resulted in a reduction of wages and benefits. Between 1995 and 2000 nearly seven million workers were displaced due to a mass layoffs or closings and a third of such displaced workers came from the manufacturing sector.[65] Surveys of such displaced workers indicate that they faced a reduction of wages on average of 13% when they found new employment, generally in the service sector. Average wages in the service sector are only 77% of those in manufacturing.[66]

Shifts in employment opportunity associated with high capital mobility and trade deficits, have had an impact on real wages. After falling or stagnating for most of the past decade, real hourly wages increased somewhat during the late 1990s boom period. However, real wages in manufacturing industries, which are where the bulk of trade activity has been, only increased by 1% during the decade, compared to 7 % in retail and 8 % in services. And whereas service sector workers saw greater wage growth, their absolute wages were significantly lower than in manufacturing. While manufacturing wages are on average $14.38 per hour, the wages in industries where many displaced factory workers are now working are much lower. Food store workers ($9.38); hotel and motel workers ($9.65); food service workers ($6.91); health service workers ($9.02); building service workers ($9.23) are examples.

It is important to note that wages at this level do not begin to pay enough to maintain even a very basic standard of living. Research on such living wages levels suggests that in a city like Chicago, a family with one wage earner and two children would need to make $18 per hour and work enough hours to earn $35,000 per year (about 37 hours per week for 52 weeks).[67]

Some workers who have been displaced have ended up earning the legislated minimum wage, which some lawmakers have fought to keep low, based on the argument that U.S. workers need to be "globally competitive." For example, one year after NAFTA went into effect, former House Speaker Newt Gingrich fought against a proposed minimum wage hike, arguing that it would widen the gap too much between U.S. and Mexican wages. This type of thinking at least partly explains the fact that the current federal minimum wage of $5.15 per hour is 27 percent lower in real terms than it was in 1963, when it was at a high point. Moreover, today's $5.15 per hour is even below the official government poverty level ($5.75 and $11,522 per year). Thus, a worker relying on the present minimum wage is likely to be homeless and hungry.

### Income Distribution

One result of workers losing ground in wages has been rising income inequality. The stagnation of wages at the lower end of the labor market and the shift generally in the distribution of employment has contributed to a redistribution of income from the poor and middle income to higher income groups. The rich got richer and the poor poorer during the 1990s. During that decade the richest 5% of the population increased their share of total family income in the U.S. by nearly 3%, while the poorest 20% of the population lost about 4% of their share. An overall index of income inequality shows that between 1990 and 2000 inequality increased by about 3.5 %.[68]

### Health Care Benefits

Wage figures also mask the situation with benefits. Increased health care costs combined with the increased power of employers to use threats of relocating have left many U.S. workers with dwindling coverage. The real value of health care and pension benefits declined from 1990 to 2000 from $3.93 to $3.58 per hour. And benefits' share of total compensation also declined during this period from 19.4% to 17.4%. Even these averages don't begin to reflect the crisis in health care due to workers not only absorbing cut backs in previous benefits but also being forced out of benefit paying jobs and into jobs without benefits. Since 1988 there has been a significant drop in the percentage of workers covered by employer health plans from 65% to 60%. For part time workers, only 17% are covered and only 7.4 of temporary help agency workers are covered.[69]

### Contingent Work

A specific aspect of the shifts in employment distribution and the stagnation of wages is the rise of contingent labor. As employment shifts out of manufacturing to lower quality service and retail employment, there has also been a rise in contingent work that includes both part time work and temporary work. Non permanent and less than full time workers now constitute 30% of the U.S. workforce and that percentage is growing.[70] Such "nonstandard" jobs include part time work, temporary agency work, on-call work, day labor and self-employment. Workers in all of these nonstandard arrangements are more likely than full time workers, permanent workers to receive low and poverty level wages. Their average wages are lower. As noted they have far lower health benefit coverage. Wage penalties compared to full time, permanent workers range from 10-18%.

Temporary agency work, a part of the contingent work category, is a very small part of the total labor force that includes standard work arrangements (2.3%). But temporary help agency employment is also one of the fastest growing parts of the economy increasing four-fold since the early 1980s and the Bureau of Labor Statistics projects that growth will continue into the next decade. These jobs are among the worst in the U.S. economy paying the lowest wages and benefits and being highly unstable.[71]

### Homelessness

There is considerable evidence that homelessness is one result of the lack of living wage jobs. Estimates of the number of homeless are difficult due to the fact that this population cannot be easily surveyed and there is no standard definition for the term. Nonetheless surveys have estimated how many people are homeless on a given night and what the composition of the homeless is. Also by comparing the demand for shelter space over time, there are estimates of the rate of growth of homelessness. According to the National Coalition for the Homeless, on a given night there are presently about 700,000 homeless people and that approximately 2 million people experience homelessness during the year. Moreover, homelessness has been growing throughout the late 1980s and the 1990s. Studies of 11 communities and 4 states found that shelter capacity more than doubled in 9 communities and tripled in the other two. Most importantly the incidence of homelessness for families, people who are working, and children is growing. Families with children now constitute 40% of all people who become homeless. Children under 18 constitute 18% of homeless people. Approximately 22% of the homeless are employed. It has been estimated that the average minimum wage worker would have to work 87 hours a week to rent a two-bedroom apartment using 30% of his or her income. In the Chicago region a recent survey of 1,300 homeless revealed 54% were from the suburbs, 39% were employed, and half said that the loss of a job was the primary reason for being homeless.[72]

### Incarceration

Rising incarceration rates during the 1990s is an indicator that the economic system is not working as it should. During a period when crime rates fell by 10%, the nation's prison population grew by 3%. The U.S. now has one of the highest incarceration rates in the world, 481 per 100,000 population. Canada, by comparison has only 129.[73] The use of prison labor is growing with more than 80,000 inmates holding traditional jobs with private companies or government. The number of prison inmates employed by the Federal Government program is up 14% over the last two years. The government prison labor industry now has more than $600 million in annual sales and is seeking to expand even further.

### Finance and Investment

NAFTA's Chapters 11 and 14 prohibit practically all regulations of the flow of money and investment throughout the region. Investors from the NAFTA nations can make portfolio investments in one another's countries and pull those investments out without warning or without impediment of any sort. Foreign direct investment is likewise unrestricted because NAFTA prohibits the use of performance requirements such as local content rules that would enhance the local economic benefits of these investments. From a U.S. perspective this unregulated flow of money into and out of the other NAFTA nations has served to make U.S. capital and business more mobile within the region. As a result it has contributed to the problems associated with highly mobile capital that have been enumerated earlier such as the use of the threat of shutdown in labor negotiations and the ability to move jobs to lower wage areas.

### Immigration

One of the promises of NAFTA was that it would help Mexico and lower pressures to immigrate to the U.S. This has not happened. Between 1991 and 2000 the number of persons declared "illegal aliens" and deported from the United States grew by 51% to 1,814,729.[74] 95% of these deportees were from Mexico. Between 1998 and 2001 legal Mexican migration to the U.S. increased by 40% and in 2001 205,000 Mexicans came to this country. Mexicans constitute 26% of all legal migration into the U.S.

One important aspect of immigration is the extent to which Mexico and other Latin American and Caribbean nations (LAC) depend on money earned by immigrants (remittances). Remittances from LAC nations have increased at an annual rate of

10% and reached a total of $20 billion in 2000. The growth in Mexico, which constitutes 54% of all LAC migrants, has also been significant. In 1977 estimated remittances from Mexico stood at less than $1 billion. But by 1997 the figure was over $5 billion and estimates for 2001 suggest that the figure is now over $9 billion.[75]

Civil rights of Mexican migrants to the United States are a growing problem. Mexicans trying to enter the country without documents are subject to very harsh conditions that have often proved fatal. Also, they are treated roughly by border guards if they get caught while entering. Efforts in border states to limit the rights of immigrants have had an impact on living and working conditions of many migrants. Prior to the incident of September 11, 2001 there was a move to legalize the status of migrants but this has been taken off the table by President Bush.

## IV. "Free Trade" and the Business Cycle

Generally, depending on the availability of data, we have been focusing our analysis on the decade of the 1990's. One reason for this is to avoid impacts of the business cycle on the trends we discuss. Recession has recently hit all three NAFTA nations hard. While the U.S. is technically out of official recession (defined as two consecutive quarters of negative GDP growth, unemployment rates continue to be high and economic growth itself low. In the U.S. the 2001 recession and its sluggish aftermath (termed by economists a "jobless recovery" has reversed even the minimal gains due to the rapid economic growth and low unemployment in the latter part of the 1990s. Moreover the nature of the recession and the lack of any significant recovery are in part attributable to the so-called "free trade" regime. This is true for several reasons.

As we have documented earlier, the so-called "free trade" regime including NAFTA has facilitated a shift from manufacturing to lower paying service jobs or to temporary and/or part time "contingent work." The shift in jobs to lower wage areas has not only depressed wages in the U.S. but has created a global system of production in which goods are produced by cheaper labor. Some economists have argued that this is more "efficient." But it has also reduced the ability of consumers to buy the products of the system. During the 1990's in the U.S. this slack was taken up by consumer debt. In 1979, household debt as a percentage of annual personal income was at 63%. By 1979 the percentage had grown to 76% and by 1997 it had reached 85%. Between 1990 and 2000 credit card debt grew from $432 billion to $1,173 billion. This growth as a percentage of personal disposable income was over 61%. With the recession of the early 2000s this level of household debt plus mounting levels of government debt has acted as a drag on any recovery from the business cycle.

The same is true of the debt incurred by the growing negative balance of trade. Spending more on imports than exports in the U.S. as a whole has meant that during the 1990's the U.S. has had to borrow money from outside the U.S. to make up the difference. This has meant that we have been accumulating a debt with the rest of the world that amounts to 23% of our gross domestic product, which is over $400 billion a year. Some economists project that this figure will grow to 40% by 2006.[76] One thing that has enabled this to go on was that the dollar was over-valued (and still is) relative to other currencies. But as the recession picked up steam, there has been less demand for U.S. assets so the value of the dollar is slipping making imports more costly and exports cheaper. The slip, however, has not been enough to lower trade deficits but it has been along with the deficit itself a drag on recovery.

One result of lower purchasing power and high debt has been a reduced capability to purchase products. During the 1990's, however, the boom in exports and high capital mobility caused U.S. businesses to increase production capacity. This contradiction has resulted in massive over capacity (capacity to produce exceeding the demand for the products). During the 1990s the capacity to produce semi conductors in the U.S. increased by over 5,000%. But since May 2000 the use of this capacity has declined from 99% to 67%. In the case of communications equipment the increase in capacity was 891% and its use since May 2000 has declined from 88% to 50%. Similar figures for virtually every major export industry in the U.S. attest to the glut in capacity, which is acting as a drag on jobs in future.[77]

## V. NAFTA and Inequality: The Case of U.S. African-Americans and Latinos

Historic discrimination against people of color in the U.S. has resulted in considerable inequalities between these groups and white society. Moreover, economic problems generally hit these groups the hardest as they are the most vulnerable in the population. This has certainly been the case during the decade of the 1990's at a time when there has been vigorous economic growth, but as we have seen above, working people saw wages stagnate, health care benefits decline, massive job dislocation and re-entry into the labor market in lower wage service jobs. In this sense, the problems associated with NAFTA and related trade agreements described above have exacerbated inequalities between people of color and white society.

To begin with, the gap in wages generally between white workers on the one hand and those of both African Americans and Latinos has widened. In 1990 the difference between white median family income and that of African Americans and Latinos was $12,645 and $18,901 respectively. By 2000 these gaps had widened to $14,249 and 19,748. The same was true for median weekly earnings. The gap in 1990 for African Americans was $95 per week and for Latinos it was $120. By 2000 these gaps had increased to $123 and $195. Thus the general point raised earlier about growing income inequality is even greater when it comes to African Americans and Latinos.

Similarly there is a gap in access to health care benefits that has been maintained throughout the decade of the 1990s. In 2000 67% of whites had access to health care benefits while the figures for African Americans and Latinos was 60% and 45% respectively. Again the general problems discussed earlier about access to health care and other benefits, applies even more to these groups.

One reason for these growing gaps has to do with the massive job dislocation that is associated with negative trade balances and highly mobile capital. African Americans and Latinos are often the first to be unemployed during episodes of dislocation and it takes them longer to find alternative employment. Between January, 1999 and December 2001, for example, nearly 10 million workers were displaced due to plant closings, layoffs or the abolishment of their position or shift. About half of this displacement was due to plant closings or moves and about a quarter was due to layoffs. 16% of these displaced workers were African American and 14% were Latinos. By January, 2002 20% of white workers were still unemployed. But 30% of African American displaced workers and 26% of Latinos were unemployed.

As a result, unemployment rates of both African Americans and Latinos have been consistently higher during the 1990-2000 period. In 1990 the African American unemployment rate was 3 times greater than the rate for whites (15.1% as opposed to 4.8%). Latinos had a rate of 9.3%, which was two times higher. By 2000 with strong economic growth the gap narrowed slightly but was still significant. African Americans had a rate that was more than twice that of whites (7.6% vs. 3.5%). And Latinos had a rate that was 1.5 times that of whites (5.7%). So even in the best of times these groups did poorly. During the current recession it is likely that the gap will widen once more. As of December, 2002, the unemployment rates for white workers was 5.1%. For African Americans and Latinos the rate was 11.5% and 7.9% respectively. These gaps are likely understated since unemployment rates do not include so-called "discouraged workers" who are unemployed but who have given up looking for work.

But the reason for the growing gap in living standards between whites and people of color is more than unemployment. There is strong evidence to conclude that the general point made earlier about dislocated workers ending up in lower wage and benefit jobs applies even more to African Americans and Latinos. This can be seen in the fact that they are over represented in some of the worst industries in the labor market that are also the fastest growing in terms of jobs. For example, while African Americans constitute 12% of the labor force, they account for 23% of temporary help workers, 24% of security guards, 16% of building service workers and 15% of health service workers. While Latinos represent 11% of the total labor force they constitute 27% of building service workers, 11% of temporary help workers, and 12% of retail service workers. On the other hand in the Finance, Insurance and Real Estate industry (FIRE), which is also a rapid growth industry but with higher pay and benefits, these groups are under-represented with 11% and 7% respectively.

The end result is that more African Americans and Latinos have fallen into poverty and/or have been incarcerated. The average poverty rate for whites between 1999 and 2000 was 7.5%. For African Americans that rate was 23.1% and for Latinos it was 22.1%. While African American's and Latinos constitute 25% of the U.S. population they make up 61% of the homeless. 49% of homeless people are African American while 12% are Latino. In the case of incarceration rates, in 1999 11% of all black males in their 20s and 30s were in prison or jail. The comparable figure for Latinos was 4% and for whites it was 1.5%. Presently African Americans and Latinos make up 62% of the prison population compared to 25% of the entire population of the U.S. In the case of African American women, they are incarcerated in state institutions at rates 10-35 times greater than white women. Latino youth are incarcerated at rates 7-17 times greater than white youth.

## Other Sources

Unless otherwise noted labor market data on employment and wages is taken from 2000 Census Labor Force, Employment and Earnings Report. Layoff statistics come from Bureau of Labor Statistics Mass Layoff Report (www.bls.gov). Data on NAFTA Trade Adjustment Assistance comes from U.S. Department of Labor Employment and Training Administration (www.doleta.gov/tradeact/taa/ntaa).

# Chapter 4
# NAFTA in Canada: The Era of a Supra-Constitution

John W. Foster [78] and John Dillon[79]

For Canada, NAFTA, along with its predecessor, the Canada-U.S. Free Trade Agreement (CUFTA), represents the era of a supra-constitution, a limiting framework which not only binds Canada with its southern neighbors, but limits democracy at home by prioritizing and protecting market dominance and the rights of property holders and investors.

There have long been advocates of economic integration who, without proposing significant modifying structures of political governance, have argued that FTAs lead inevitably to customs unions, common markets and ultimately effective political unions. Before the CUFTA, United States Trade Representative, Clayton Yeutter uttered an oft-recited comment on the bilateral agreement: "The Canadians don't understand what they signed. In twenty years, they will be sucked into the US economy. … Free-trade talks with Canada shouldn't be an end in themselves, but should ultimately lead to the creation of a North American common market. Free trade is just the first step in a process leading to the creation of a single North American economy." Fifteen years before him, a prescient Canadian foreign minister wrote, "free trade tends towards a full customs union and economic union as a matter of internal logic. A Canada–U.S. free-trade area would almost certainly do likewise. If this were to happen, Canada would be obliged to seek political union with its superpower neighbor."

NAFTA's ninth anniversary provided the occasion for enthusiastic mutual congratulations among the government leaders who signed the original accord – George H.W. Bush, Carlos

Salinas and Brian Mulroney. Beyond the glow of the candles of celebration, however, deep issues emerge. The logic of the integration process unleashed by the agreement and its predecessor, the CUFTA, poses new challenges for the citizens of Canada and a warning for other peoples contemplating whether to join a Free Trade Area of the Americas.

External political factors, perhaps unimagined by the architects of NAFTA, have emerged in the past two years to complicate relations. A multilateralist Canada now confronts a unilateralist, interventionist and aggressive neighbor. The United States is more sensitive to real and alleged threats to its security and interests. Those who link political differences to economic consequences argue the only path is to eradicate political autonomy or divergence.

The debate over NAFTA and further trade and investment negotiations has entered a new and deeper phase.

## I. NAFTA: The Economics

The era of Canada-U.S. free trade has been marked by a phenomenal growth in commerce between the two countries. When CUFTA negotiations began in 1985, bilateral trade was valued at US$116 billion; by 2002 this figure had reached over US$420 billion. Between 1989, when the CUFTA came into effect, and 2002, Canadian exports to the United States rose by 221 while imports from the United States increased by 162 percent.

While politicians and media pundits are prone to point to these figures as evidence of NAFTA's "success", such crude mercantilist measures do not conform to the actual economic rationale for free trade. One of the arguments for undertaking a "leap of faith" into free trade was supposedly to counter an alarming decline in Canada's rate of economic growth. In terms of increases in GDP per capita, which is by itself a rather dubious measure of genuine progress, Canada's economy had grown at an average rate of 1.9 percent per year during the eight years prior to the implementation of the CUFTA. During the first five years under CUFTA real GDP growth per capita was actually negative, averaging -0.4 percent a year. As we shall see below, this decline in the growth rate is linked to the Bank of Canada's tough monetary policy, which was also a consequence of an unannounced side deal attached to the CUFTA. For the free-trade era as a whole, 1989-2002, real per capita growth averaged 1.6 percent a year, which is still below its pre-CUFTA rate.

Putting aside crude measures of export performance and growth in GDP, the actual economic rationale for free trade is based on the supposition "that increases in two-way trade would boost productivity through greater specialization and the workings of comparative advantage.[80] Put more starkly "the cold shower of increased competition would force Canadian firms to adopt new technology quickly or fail." Furthermore, and most importantly, increases in productivity were expected to translate into higher wages and rising living standards.

However, the productivity and wage figures tell a different story than what the trade data might suggest. For the purpose of this analysis, it is necessary to break the data down into two periods that roughly correspond to the era of bilateral free trade under CUFTA and the NAFTA eras.

 Over the period 1989-1993, average hourly labor productivity in the business sector in Canada grew at an annual rate of 0.6 percent, which was less than half of its rate of growth over the previous eight years (1981-1988), when productivity rose by 1.6 percent per year. Over the same years (1989-1993) real, that is, inflation-adjusted, hourly wages in Canada rose by only 0.2 percent per year, which was less than half the 0.5 percent rate of growth of real wages over the previous eight years.

Productivity growth regained and even exceeded its pre-CUFTA rate over the years 1994-2002, when average hourly productivity went up by 2.1 percent a year. But real wages only rose at an annual rate of 0.4 percent over those years. Thus, real wage gains consistently lagged behind increases in productivity throughout the free-trade era, meaning that employers, not workers, reaped the benefits of higher output per hour.

An examination of the contrast between U.S., Mexican and Canadian productivity increases in the key manufacturing sector from 1993 to June of 2002, a period of economic recovery, helps to explain why Canadian living standards fell behind those in the United States. As shown in Figure 4-1, over that period the cumulative increase in Canadian output per hour was only 14.52 percent, while the increase in the United States amounted to 51.98 percent and, in Mexico, 53 percent. As the graph also shows, labor costs, measured in U.S. dollars, borne by manufacturing firms actually fell in all three countries, further evidence that productivity gains were not passed on to workers.

In the year before the CUFTA was implemented, manufacturing productivity in Canada stood at 83 percent of the U.S. level. By 2000 it was only 65 percent. Thus the productivity gap widened, rather than narrowed as promised by the proponents of free trade. One of the reasons for the widening productivity gap is the dominance of foreign transnational corporations in Canadian manufacturing. Foreign corporations typi-

**Figure 4-1**
**Manufacturing Productivity and Labour Costs**
Cumulative Annual % Changes '93-Jun'02

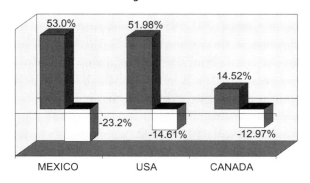

cally invest 67 percent less than domestic firms in industrial research and development.[81]

An Industry Canada study found that lower labor productivity explains 96 percent of the gap between Canadian and U.S. living standards during the 1990s.[82] At the beginning of the 1990s the personal income of the average Canadian stood at 87 percent of his or her U.S. counterpart. By the turn of the century it had fallen to 78 percent, with most of the decline occurring in the first half of the decade.[83]

**Investment**

The promoters of free trade hoped that the CUFTA would lead to new foreign direct investment (FDI) in Canada and the expansion of U.S.-owned branch plants. During the first seven years under the CUFTA, U.S. FDI in Canada grew by a modest C$36.8 billion before taking off again over the next seven years (1996-2002), when a further C$102 billion in net FDI from the United States accrued in Canada. But most of this investment involved takeovers of Canadian firms, not new "greenfield" investments. For the period June 1985 through June 2002, there were a total of 10,052 foreign takeovers of Canadian companies, with 6,437 of them by U.S. corporations. Of all the new foreign direct investment in Canada over the period, an extraordinary 96.6 percent was for takeovers and only 3.4 percent for new businesses.[84] Moreover, many of these takeovers were financed through borrowing within Canada.

In 1989 U.S. foreign direct investment (FDI) in Canada accounted for 12 percent of Canadian Gross Domestic Product. By 2001 it was equivalent to 20 percent of all goods and services produced in Canada.

Meanwhile there was a marked increase in Canadian FDI in the United States, showing a pattern of disinvestment from Canada. By 2002 Canadians held approximately US$133 billion worth of FDI in the United States, a figure three times what it was in 1990. Does this indicate that foreign investors, led by Canadians, are taking control of key U.S. industries? Not at all. Mel Hurtig explains. "There is not one single industry in the United States, not one, that is majority-foreign-owned and/or foreign-controlled, by anyone, let alone Canadians. Only two of scores of U.S. industries are remotely close, chemicals and book publishing, which are about one-third foreign."[85] As of 1999 Canadians owned less than 0.6 percent of U.S. industrial investment and ranked sixth among foreign investors in the United States. Moreover, between 30 percent and 40 percent of "Canadian" investment abroad isn't Canadian at all. Rather it is foreign investment by foreign corporations located in Canada.

Despite the growth in Canadian investment in the United States, there have been more than four times as many U.S. acquisitions of Canadian firms since NAFTA came into effect. Over the years 1995-2001, U.S. corporations bought out 3,008 Canadian firms, while Canadians took over 697 U.S. companies.[86]

### Job losses and monetary policy

In describing its "success", NAFTA boosters credit the agreement with increased employment and prosperity in all three countries. During NAFTA's first nine years, employment in Canada grew by 19 percent, representing a gain of 2.7 million new jobs. However, as shown below, fewer than half these new jobs were full-time. Moreover, this apparently rosy period of Canadian job gains under NAFTA has to be set against a prior six-year period of job losses under the CUFTA. Between 1988 and 1994 Canada lost 334,000 manufacturing jobs, equivalent to 17 percent of total manufacturing employment in the year before CUFTA took effect. How does one account for this initial job loss and later job gains? Were they all due to tariff reductions under the CUFTA and NAFTA?

A detailed sectoral study by Daniel Trefler of the University of Toronto shows that tariff reductions accounted for about one-third of the job losses during the period 1988-1996. This was especially true in sectors such as clothing manufacturing, where workers are mostly immigrant women with few other employment options besides toiling in unregistered sweatshops for less than the minimum wage. The other two-thirds of job losses were the result of the severe recession provoked by the Bank of Canada's high interest-rate policy. These same high interest rates were responsible for the overvaluation of the Canadian dollar relative to its U.S. counterpart.

It was only after interest rates came down in 1994 that employment revived and Canada's bilateral current account balance with the United States turned from deficits to surpluses, as shown in Figure 4-2 The chart tracks Canada's current account balance with the United States, a measure that takes into account not only trade but also other bilateral payments for such things as services, travel and interest and dividends. The graph shows how the bilateral current account balance is directly related to the value of the Canadian dollar in relation to the U.S. greenback.

When the Canadian dollar was below US$0.78 over the period 1984-1987 Canada had a surplus on its current account,

**Figure 4-2**
**Canada's Current Account Balance with the U.S. and Exchange Rate**

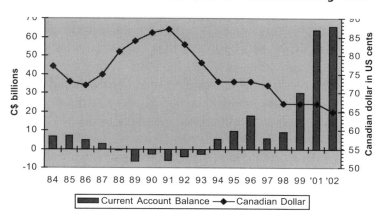

as a low dollar makes exports cheaper, imports more expensive and serves to lure tourists to vacation in Canada. When the dollar rose above 78 cents over the years 1988-1993, the current account fell into deficit, only to return to a surplus position after 1994 when the dollar declined again. The high dollar period, 1988-1993, corresponds to the second term of the Mulroney government and the advent of the CUFTA. There is strong evidence that the rise in the value of the dollar was directly linked to an unannounced side deal that Mulroney made with the Reagan administration. During the negotiation of the CUFTA, the powerful U.S. National Manufacturers Association lobbied Treasury Secretary James Baker to use the trade agreement "to eliminate the exchange rate advantage gained by Canadian producers" over their U.S. competitors during the decade before CUFTA.[87]

Subsequently, Baker told a U.S. Senate Foreign Relations Committee hearing that the revaluation of the Canadian dollar was the price that Canada would have to pay for admission into the Group of Seven industrial countries. (There had been only G5 – France, Germany, the U.K., the US and Japan- before Canada and Italy joined.) Later a former Mulroney cabinet minister, Sinclair Stevens, told the *Toronto Star* that there indeed had been a side deal to revalue the Canadian dollar upward.

The mechanism that the Mulroney government used to keep the dollar overvalued was the high interest-rate policy of the Bank of Canada. These same high interest rates brought on a severe recession during the early 1990s. Thus the increase in employment after 1994 had less to do with the advent of NAFTA that year than with the lower interest rates and devaluation of the dollar that stimulated economic recovery. This conclusion is reinforced by studies by Industry Canada that credit strong bilateral trade growth to a lower Canadian dollar and strong US domestic growth rates rather than to NAFTA. These government studies say that NAFTA should be credited with only nine percent of growth in Canadian exports and only two percent growth in imports from the United States in real terms.

## Labor and flexibilization of the work force

Although the Mulroney government sold free trade to Canadians on a promise that it would create "jobs, jobs, jobs", the high interest-rate policy actually led to a decline in employment and a severe recession over the years 1991-1993. Thus Canada's official unemployment rate went up from an average of 7.8 percent over 1988-1990 to 11 percent during 1991-1993. Between 1995 and 2001, unemployment averaged 8.6 percent. During the first thirteen years under CAFTA and NAFTA, Canada created less than half as many full-time jobs as during the previous thirteen years.

However, these figures do not tell the whole story, as many of the jobs created during the NAFTA period have been part-time, insecure jobs with few benefits, especially for women. A study on labor-market conditions in Canada under NAFTA found that "Part-time workers – overwhelmingly women – earn just two-thirds the wages of equivalent full-time workers, and less than 20 percent receive benefits from their employers. Increasingly, part-time work has become more and more casual, with hours in sectors such as retail trade, restaurants and hotels highly variable from one week to the next."[88] There has also been growth in temporary work. In 1991, 5.0 percent of workers held temporary jobs. By 1996 this figure had risen to 11.6 percent of total employment. Similarly, self-employment grew by 15 percent between 1991 and 1995, contributing about one-half of all "job" growth in the 1990s.

The year 2002 was marked by an extraordinary increase of 560,000 jobs in Canada. But 40 percent of these jobs were part-time and another 17 percent were self-employed. Thus, while the overall employment statistics look better, the process of creating a more flexible workforce continues. Furthermore, the productivity gap continued to widen as Canada had little productivity growth in 2002, while the United States made huge gains in output per hour largely by shedding 100,000 jobs.[89]

## Social programs

Since the beginning of the free-trade era, Canada's own business elite has argued that Canadian social programs would have to conform to the generally inferior U.S. levels in order to maintain competitiveness. As early as 1980, Laurent Thibault, who later became president of the Canadian Manufacturers Association, told a Senate committee: "It is a simple fact that, as we ask our industries to compete toe to toe with American industry ... we in Canada are obviously forced to create the same conditions in Canada that exist in the U.S., whether it is the unemployment insurance scheme, Workmens' (sic) Compensation, the cost of government, the level of taxation, whatever."

Indeed in April of 1989, just four months after the implementation of the CUFTA, the Conservative government brought down what became known as its "free-trade budget". It included cuts to Unemployment Insurance, Old Age Security and federal transfers to provinces for health care and education. This pattern of spending cuts continued throughout the mandate of the Conservative government. It was accelerated after the Liberals were elected in 1993 and especially pronounced in the watershed budget of 1995 which included C$29 billion in spending cuts over three years.

While real per capita hourly wages rose slowly during the free-trade era (as noted above), cutbacks in social transfers meant that Canadians' personal disposable income actually fell during the first decade under free trade. Whereas personal disposable income had grown by 3 percent a year over the period 1973-1981 and by 1.1 percent annually over 1981-89, it declined by 0.3 percent a year between 1989 and 1999.[90]

The clearest example of the downward harmonization of Canadian social policy is what happened to unemployment insurance. The system has been cut by both Conservative and Liberal governments to conform to the lower standards prevailing in the United States. Whereas in 1989, 87 percent of the unemployed in Canada qualified for insurance (as compared to 52 percent in the United States), by 2001 only 39 percent of unemployed Canadians could collect Employment Insurance. Moreover, more women lost employment insurance protection than men, as they more frequently work part time and enter and leave the workforce more often due to childcare responsibilities.

Neither is Canada's public health-care system protected. Although Annex II to NAFTA supposedly provides an exemption for Medicare and other social services, its safeguards are of uncertain and limited value. The NAFTA safeguards only cover services "established or maintained for a public purpose". Many trade lawyers believe that this vague language does not protect Canada's health-care system where private practitioners work within a publicly administered system. Moreover, the reservation provides no protection whatsoever from investors claiming compensation for measures "tantamount to expropriation" under NAFTA's investor-state mechanism described elsewhere in this publication. If a U.S. insurance firm or homecare supplier wants to sue Canada for losses, or even potential losses, incurred due to the expansion of public health insurance to cover new services, it is free to do so.

The government-appointed Romanow Commission on the Future of Health Care has confirmed what critics of free-trade agreements have long maintained, "Once there is a significant foreign presence engaged in for-profit delivery of health care services, any attempt to restrict its access to the market in the future may result in relatively high compensation claims." NAFTA threatens Canada's ability to extend Medicare into new areas such as home care and pharmacare because Canada might have to compensate foreign investors for lost market share. The deterrent effect of possibly having to compensate foreign investors is illustrated by what happened to the New Democratic Party government's promise to establish public auto insurance in Ontario such as already exists in Manitoba and British Columbia. One of the chief reasons why Premier Bob Rae backed away from this promise was the fear that U.S.-owned insurance companies would demand and win millions of dollars worth of compensation under NAFTA.

### Trade disputes continue to harm Canada

When Canada first undertook to negotiate free trade with the United States, the Mulroney government claimed that the purpose was to win exemptions for Canada from U.S. anti-dumping and countervailing duty measures. But Canada never achieved this goal. Instead Canada remains subject to arbitrary U.S. actions such as the punitive U.S. duty on Canadian softwood lumber exports. This 27 percent tariff was imposed in 2002 because the U.S. lumber industry alleges that their Canadian competitors are unfairly subsidized. Canadian lumber firms pay lower fees to cut timber on publicly owned lands than U.S. companies pay for cutting rights on privately owned wood lots. So far, Canadian exporters have been forced to pay about $1 billion (Canadian) in duties. One possible solution under discussion would involve Canadian provinces selling more timber at U.S.-style public auctions. This would constitute yet another modification of Canada's historical preference for public administration of natural resources to conform with the U.S. predilection for free-enterprise management.

Instead of winning an exemption from U.S. contingency protection laws (anti-dumping and countervailing duty measures), all that Canada won was a provision that special panels would examine whether U.S. laws were correctly applied in the first place. Thus the rulings and precedents accumulated by CUFTA and NAFTA adjudicatory panels are based on U.S. trade law. Canadian trade researcher Scott Sinclair comments that the United States, "can change these laws unilaterally to negate the effect of an unfavorable panel ruling." More importantly, before the advent of CUFTA and NAFTA, Canada opposed U.S. charges that its agricultural supports, regional development and transportation programs were "trade-distorting". Under CUFTA, disputes in each of these cases were settled in favor of the USA and Canada's participation in CUFTA appeared to sanction these decisions, weakening future stances.

U.S. actions in 2002, including the renewed imposition of the punitive 27 percent duty on Canadian softwood lumber, along with the U.S. Farm Bill, have exacerbated irritation.

## Agriculture

Canadian farmers' experience with free trade clearly demonstrates how more trade does not necessarily translate into more prosperity. In a review of Canadian farm experience since the approval of the bilateral CUFTA in 1988, the National Farmers Union notes that agri-food exports have almost tripled, but net farm income adjusted for inflation is down 24 percent. Over the same period farm debt has doubled with the result that interest payments on that debt are almost as high as net farm income. In other words, the banks make nearly as much money off of farming as the families who do all the hard work.

Some 16 percent of Canadian farmers have been forced off the land. There were 2,400 fewer jobs in the agri-food processing industry in 2002 than in 1988. The number of independent hog farmers has declined by 66 percent, while corporate production has taken over. The farmgate price for hogs rose by just two percent and the wages paid to workers in packing plants went up just three percent between 1988 and 2002, while the price of pork chops in the grocery store rose by 39 percent. Farmer-owned co-ops, once dominant in the grain trade and in dairy processing, have been taken over or marginalized.

The National Farmers Union concluded in 2002 that free-trade agreements, "may increase trade but, much more importantly, they dramatically alter the relative size and market power of the players in the agri-food production chain…Free trade helps Cargill and Monsanto, not farmers."

### Broader social impact and growing inequality

The broader social impact of NAFTA is captured by Ken Traynor of the Canadian Environment Law Association who comments, "The old issue of who gets what even when overall 'economic efficiency' may have been enhanced is worth examining. Consider moving brassière manufacture from Cambridge, Ontario to Juárez on the Mexican border. $8 per hour wages paid to women in Cambridge to produce brassieres sold for $20…gets spent in the immediate vicinity of their homes, gets taxed and the firm generates local municipal taxes too. With NAFTA and a shift of production to the *maquilas*, only $2 of the $64 per day wages saved goes to the women in Mexico and almost none of the municipal and other taxes are paid in Mexico. The $62 per day per worker gets reallocated to Exxon for fuel to ship things around, to road transport companies, to brokers, and to the company itself and the spending circle of these guys is very different than that of the women displaced. And where the money circulates does matter," Traynor concludes, "especially to the women in this example."

Canada has become a noticeably more unequal society in the free-trade era. Real incomes declined for the majority of Canadians in the 1990s. Statistics Canada notes that, despite a slight three-year rise in Canadian median income, the 1999 figure is actually $1,100, or two percent lower, than in 1990. While everything cannot all be blamed on CUFTA and NAFTA, the downward pressure on wages, flexibilization of the workforce and cutbacks to social transfer payments described above certainly contributed to rising inequality.

Neo-liberal economic policies, including free trade, have contributed to a markedly more unequal distribution of wealth defined here as all personal assets minus all personal debts. Over the period 1984-1999 (two years in which Statistics Canada conducted two of its infrequent reviews of wealth distribution) the poorest 40 percent of Canadians saw their share of total wealth fall from owning 1.8 percent of all personal assets to just 1.1 percent. Over the same period the richest 10 percent of the population saw their net worth rise from 51.8 percent of all wealth to 55.7 percent. In terms of average dollar wealth per family unit (in constant 1999 dollars, that is adjusted for inflation) the poorest 40 percent of Canadians saw their average wealth fall from C$5,918 in 1984 to just C$4,800 in 1999. In contrast the wealthiest decile increased their average family assets from C$667,485 to C$980,903 over the same years, 1984-1999.

The closest comparable U.S. figures show a decline in average family wealth for the poorest 40 percent from US$4,700 in 1983 to just US$1,100 in 1998. Over the same period the richest 20 percent of family units in the United States increased their average family assets from US$864,500 to US$1,126,700.[91]

## II. Getting in Deeper: Advocates and Arguments about "Deep Integration"

The economic inter-penetration between Canada and the United States, which was quickened by CUFTA and NAFTA, has led to a new stage of business and media pressure for what is commonly referred to as "deep integration". As predicted twenty or more years ago by critics and opponents, "free" trade brings much else in its wake.

Canada's dependence on trade with the United States has doubled since the advent of CUFTA. Measured as a share of GDP, Canada's trade within the NAFTA zone has grown from 30 percent of GDP to 60 percent. Since Canada's trade with the United States is 45 times greater than with Mexico, almost all of this expansion is due to bilateral trade with the United

States. Meanwhile, over the last decade Canada's trade with the rest of the world did not grow at all despite the general process of economic integration globally.

After trade liberalization comes pressures to consider a customs union, a currency union or dollarization, joint immigration and refugee policies, and closer military ties, first in terms of joint continental defense, with an agreement allowing U.S. troops to operate in Canada and later to Canadian involvement in U.S.-led wars, although not all wars, overseas. The last two years have been characterized by issues and irritants which, although they have economic consequences, are essentially related to the broader political and strategic context. At the same time, advocates of deeper integration, particularly in Canada have not been idle.

### Borders

Given the significant increase in bilateral trade, there has been a massive increase not only in cross-border traffic, but also in the priority of "border issues" in bilateral relations. Proposals for facilitation of commercial and "legitimate" human cross-border traffic were raised prior to the crisis of September 11, 2001, but became both more complex and more urgent thereafter.[92] The prominence of border issues in both Canada-U.S. and Mexico-U.S. relations is high, but the factors involved, while overlapping, are not fully identical. Nor are they looked at in precisely the same way from Washington. While trade with the United States is proportionately predominant in Canada and Mexico, trade with Canada is less singularly and urgently of issue for the United States.

The threat of U.S. border tightening following September 11 had disruptive effects in both Mexico and Canada. The Fox administration's projects regarding migration were stymied. At one border crossing (Windsor, Ontario - Detroit, Michigan) the line-up of vehicles crossing into the United States stretched 36 km., as the U.S. border officials clamped down. Canada became preoccupied with the prospect of costly border delays. Canada and the U.S. signed a "Smart Border Accord" late in 2001, with 30 points of cooperation. They agreed to station officers from each other's services in ports on each coast, as well as a series of measures to facilitate secure cross-border truck transit.

Two important programs followed in 2002: the "Free and Secure Trade" (FAST) initiative, in which private-sector companies pre-certify their commercial shipments and the drivers; and the NEXUS program, which offers express clearance for "low-risk, pre-approved travelers" at key border points and is projected to expand in terms of the number of points and may include airports in 2003.[93]

Talk continues about the development of a "continental perimeter", but in a much lower key, with ambiguity about whether it stops at the Rio Grande, is NAFTA-inclusive or extends as far as the Panama Canal.

The border forms the sharp edge of a policy wedge. A more open border implies policy harmonization in a whole series of areas, including immigration, drugs and refugee policy. In the latter case, Canada has played a historic role as a refuge for Latin Americans – Chileans, Argentines, Central Americans – escaping from the negative effects of U.S. policies on their homelands. Some of these refugees would have been persona non grata in the United States. With regard to rules, standards and regulations on the movement of goods, the President of the Conference Board of Canada proposes separate Canadian standards be maintained "only where there are compelling public policy reasons."[94]

Among the more powerful business executives in Canada, there are voices arguing for something close to a borderless future. Tom D'Aquino, President and CEO of the Canadian Council of Chief Executives, proposes transforming the Canada-U.S. border into a "shared checkpoint within the Canada-United States economic space, and a shared North American identity document."[95] Analysts James Anderson and Eric van Wincoop, in a paper prepared for the Brookings Institute Trade Forum 2001, argue for the "astonishing large" benefits of deep integration, stating that, "policies associated with borders are very costly, even in a world with low formal trade policy barriers." Canada has been seeking an exemption from U.S. legislation that looks to full exit controls by 2005, which might involve up to US$2.5 billion in expenditure to set up scanners and other extra exist-post operations, as well as US$1 billion a year to operate them. Canada is offering to hand over information collected by Canadian border guards instead.[96] It seems clear that the debate over North America's borders has just begun.

Despite the enthusiasm of a part of the Canadian business elite for a border-free relationship, there are counter-weights, including public opinion and the interests of the Canadian state as such. One U.S. analyst, after studying the border debates and examining the rhetoric of Homeland Security head Tom Ridge and Canadian Deputy Prime Minister John Manley, concludes that there is somewhat less here than meets the eye. Stephanie Golub argues that the conceptions of sovereignty at work and the need to safeguard state interests mean that the "common perimeter" has in fact been set aside because the "level of mutuality" among the two players was insufficient to sustain it.[97]

## Security

At the top of the U.S. agenda following September 11, security concerns have had a significant impact on Canada, as well. A series of directives and legislative acts – the Patriot Act, changes in the U.S. Immigration and Naturalization Service rules, the Presidential directive authorizing military tribunals – followed the September crisis, with repeated security alerts and security initiatives. These moves had ripple effects in many countries, not least in Canada.

In December 2001 the Canadian parliament enacted Bill C-36, which created new police powers including detention without charge, which enables the federal government to list individuals or organizations as "terrorist groups" and forbid contributions to their charitable organs or dealing in their property. The bill encourages citizens to inform on each other and to answer questions in open-ended investigative hearings. In short, according to Canadian Civil Liberties Association Chief Counsel, Alan Borovoy, the government gained a "plethora of powers and a paucity of safeguards." Other initiatives have followed, provoking sharp rebukes from a number of editorialists and from the government's own Privacy Commissioner.

The government, in October 2001, created an ad hoc Cabinet Committee on Public Security and Anti-Terrorism. Deputy Prime Minister John Manley took on a role of coordination leading to periodic meetings with U.S. Homeland Security head Tom Ridge that continue into 2003. In December 2001 the government committed $7.7 billion over five years to border security and anti-terrorism measures.

Pressures to harmonize Canadian refugee and immigration policy with that of the Untied States increased significantly. Canadian business and security spokespeople argued that it was necessary to ease border transit for goods and "low risk" personnel. For the United States, it was part of a vision of a "common perimeter" which included tightening up on foreign student visas to the United States, tripling the number of Border Patrol personnel, Customs Service Personnel and INS inspectors in each state along the Canadian border. Canada followed suit with Bill C-11, restricting refugee entry and bringing Canada closer to U.S. immigration and refugee practices. Then the September 2002 Safe Third Country Agreement with the United States raised cautions in many quarters as to whether Canada might be endangering its ability to fulfill commitments under the Geneva Convention Relating to the Status of Refugee.[98]

Business and right-wing political pressure for a much more aggressive Canadian engagement with security issues is couched in terms of the necessity to respond to U.S. security preoccupations. In the view of CCCE head D'Aquino, this means "vastly more" Canadian investment in defense and a new phase of cooperation with the U.S. in defending the continent.

Discussion of joint military arrangements continued through 2002. The U.S. military announced its intention to create NORTHCOM, or Northern Command, covering all its forces wherever located in North America and including geographic responsibility for Mexico and Canada. This led to a lively debate in Canada on the implications of further military integration with the United States. Some leading defense advocates argued that Canada effectively had "no choice" but to agree to long-standing U.S. demands in areas such as missile defenses and defense spending. The U.S. Ambassador has on more than one occasion pushed Canada to increase its defense investment. There continue to be a number of voices in Parliament (not least on the benches of the official opposition Alliance party) urging relatively massive increases in defense spending. The government responded with a modest but significant new commitment in its 2003 budget. With regard to the missile defense, the government continues to monitor developments without making either a positive or negative commitment, while maintaining formal opposition to the weaponization of space. Canada and the United States made public, only in August 2002, the likelihood of an agreement permitting cross-border entry of each other's troops in case of emergency.

Meanwhile, further integration in certain overseas operations has raised concern. Canadian naval forces cooperate with the United States in the Persian Gulf. An order that they should not turn over to the United States any Iraqi figures they might intercept elicited negative comment from U.S. spokespeople. This order may, in turn, have resulted from the outcry over Canadian forces in Afghanistan operating under U.S. command who turned over prisoners to the less than merciful hands of U.S. military engaged in holding prisoners at Guantanamo Bay and elsewhere in violation of Geneva conventions.

Former Canadian foreign minister, Lloyd Axworthy, has raised serious concern about the pressures for further military integration. Along with economic integration, these pressures, he argues, poses very major questions "about the degree to which we will maintain our ability to maneuver, our freedom of choice, and our ability to make judgments based upon what we calculate to be our interests and our own values."[99]

## Energy and water

The Bush Administration is an oilman's dream. Petroleum corporations based in Canada are eager to oblige Bush's emphasis on securing more U.S. energy supplies from dependable Western Hemisphere sources. Canada's Prime Minister never tires of pointing out that Canada is the United States' largest supplier of energy imports when oil, natural gas and electricity are taken together. A leaked memo from Canada's Department of Foreign Affairs and International Trade reveals that Canada, the United States and Mexico are studying the "regulatory environment for trade in oil, gas and electricity to eliminate all impediments to North American energy security."[100]

However, it is difficult for Canadians to understand what a new "deal" on energy might give the United States that it does not already have under existing FTAs. With CUFTA and NAFTA, Canada lost the ability to adequately control energy exports. Neither Canada nor Mexico can use export taxes or impose minimum prices on energy exports within North America. Moreover, Canada alone is subject to the "proportional sharing clause", which obliges Canada, in the event of a crisis, to continue exporting non-renewable resources, including petroleum, to the United State in the same proportion of total supply as was sold over the previous three years, even if such exports cause domestic shortages. Mexico refused to accept this clause in NAFTA but Canada wants it included in the FTAA.

Deep-integration advocate Wendy Dobson argues that a ten-year program of integrating natural-resource regimes in Canada and the United States would be instrumental to an overall strategic framework.[101] She argues that giving more energy security to the United States would be a model for other natural resources, including water. Journalist Murray Dobbin comments "For Canada, it's not so much an invasion as a preemptive surrender."[102]

Under NAFTA, the concept of treating water as a tradable good has gained credence. There is an increased consciousness of U.S. "thirst" and renewed talk of projects like the "Grand Canal", which would take water from James Bay all the way down to the U.S. Midwest. Recently, the premier of the easternmost Canadian province, Newfoundland, proposed to export bulk water in tankers. Canada's jurisdiction over its water supply is divided between the federal government, which is responsible for the basis of waters that cross or flow along boundaries, and provincial governments, which deal with bodies of water within their boundaries. Should Newfoundland make water a tradable "good", several NAFTA provisions would come into play:

- *national treatment,* meaning that Canada could not "discriminate" in favor of its own water users;
- *proportionality,* meaning that once exports begin, they cannot be suspended. If there are sound environmental or health reasons for reducing the flow, then it must be done in the same proportion to domestic, as well as foreign, consumers; and
- *investor/state,* which enables private corporations to sue governments for alleged injury to their interests, already in play in the form of a suit by the Sun Belt Water Inc. of Santa Barbara, California for US$10.5 million because the Gov-

ernment of British Columbia has prevented it from exporting water to California.

Among the rights and historic environment challenged by the potential of commercial bulk water exports, those of aboriginal peoples are at the forefront. The constitutional protection of Aboriginal Title and Rights includes control of resources sufficient to support and direct their lives, ensuring, aboriginal people would claim, that their access to water comes before that of non-aboriginal users.

## Dollarization

Would a common currency, either acceptance of the U.S. dollar or a new North American Monetary Unit (NAMU) be desirable for Canada? Some academics, like Queen's University Professor Thomas Courchene, argue strenuously for such a move. Courchene would not adopt the U.S. greenback directly but invent a new unit, the NAMU, equivalent to it. Business spokesperson Dale Orr, of the Canadian office of DRI-WEFA Inc., argues that a common currency would immediately lower investment barriers and lead to stronger growth in Canada and an improvement in Canada's standard of living. Canada, Courchene argues, no longer has a national economy but a series of North-South economies tied to U.S. regions. If governments do not adopt a common currency, companies will probably adopt the greenback anyway. Indeed, from 1995 to 1998 the share of U.S. dollar deposits as a percentage of total deposits in Canadian banks rose from 27 percent to 52 percent. Will Canada become the Argentina of the north?

Mario Seccareccia, writing for the Canadian Centre for Policy Alternatives, points out that dollarization will not solve the problems its proponents argue it addresses. He advises that "Canada should continue to 'go at it alone' under a flexible exchange rate regime."[103] Roy Culpeper, President of the North-South Institute, says that dollarization is unlikely. He notes:

A stronger possibility might be the "internationalization" of the U.S. Federal Reserve, that country's central bank. Thus, Canada and Mexico could become the 13th and 14th Federal Reserve Districts, akin to the districts now served by San Francisco, Kansas City or Dallas, thereby obtaining a seat at the table of the Federal Reserve. Whether such an arrangement would be palatable to Mexico or Canada, or even to the United States, is doubtful. A much more attractive arrangement, at least for the United States, would be for Mexico and Canada to unilaterally adopt the U.S. dollar, much as Ecuador, El Salvador and East Timor have done, or peg their currency at a fixed rate to the U.S. dollar, like Liberia and Panama, for example. However, the United States has made it clear to all such countries that they have no role in U.S. monetary policy. Moreover, they cannot expect the Federal Reserve to intervene to contain financial crises, as it might do in the United States. It seems doubtful that larger, more economically independent countries such as Canada and Mexico would willingly abandon their currencies in favor of such an arrangement.[104]

The Governor of the Bank of Canada, David Dodge, remains committed to a floating exchange rate, but when Mexican President Fox proposed a common North American currency while visiting Canada, Prime Minister Chretien rebuffed the proposal. The major business proponents of deep integration appear to have put dollarization to the side for the moment, probably expecting that, if ownership rules on Canadian banks are changed to allow majority U.S. ownership, and if corporations continue enlarging their cross-border transactions, it will come along eventually without the need to force the issue.

## III. Deep Integration: Strategic Bargain or Bad Deal

The call for "deep integration" in North America, or more particularly between the United States and Canada, was heard long before September 11, 2001, but became more strident and more complex as the implications of the crisis unfurled. U.S. Trade Representative Zoellick had suggested earlier in 2001 a Canadian initiative to open up the bilateral relations issue with the United States, and deep integrationists were arguing for harmonization of standards between the two countries, greater cooperation between ministries in such areas as transportation policy, competition policy and taxation, and common environmental and pharmaceutical standards. There was also a fairly loud, if hardly universal, call for dollarization.

There have been several further waves of deep-integration lobbying since September 11, 2001. In 2002, for example, major Canadian think-tanks – the CD Howe Institute, the Fraser Institute, etc. – along with the Canadian Council of Chief Executives (CCCE), argued for a "strategic initiative", sometimes called the "big idea":

> Noting that sovereignty is only meaningful when it is exercised, proponents argue Canadians should exercise it by giving it away. Taking advantage of U.S. concern for security, Canada should propose a comprehensive bargain in which an open border, harmonized policies in immigration (for eased entry of 'low risk' migrants, security, closer military cooperation, energy, etc.), would be offered in return for an end to trade remedy laws aimed at Canada, common competition policy, etc. A common currency might be put off until later, although some would prefer it as part of the package. Mexico, like a common currency, might be dealt with further down the road. Relative unanimity among elite policy think tanks and leading trade advocates emerged at a

series of conferences and strategy sessions in the spring and summer of 2002.[105]

Most advocates have concentrated on an economic deal reached at a high political level without much in the way of new institutional structures. One of the advocates, Hugh Segal of the Institute for Research on Public Policy, has argued that political institutions for a "North American Community" need to be developed with the same creativity that gave birth to the United Nations more than fifty years ago.

Some U.S. commentators reacted favorably to this Canadian business initiative. However, negotiators have failed to solve differences over trade remedy laws and countervailing duties. A five-year limit in the CUFTA on coming to agreement on these contingency protection measures passed quietly without the resolution of these key irritants and without Canada even referring to a special abrogation clause that would have allowed for the termination of CUFTA because of this failure. Others have noted that, even given U.S. security preoccupations and the focus on a "common perimeter" for North America, Canada's concerns do not get priority in Washington. Furthermore, the U.S. Congress is unlikely to cede its right to undertake actions – like passing the 2002 Farm Bill – that have seriously negative trade effects on their northern (and southern) neighbors. Similarly, the Administration and the USTR are unlikely to refrain in the future from actions to protect U.S. softwood-lumber or steel producers or other threatened interests.

In 2003 there have been two further rounds of pro-deep-integration initiatives by Canadian business figures, commencing with a salvo from the CCCE in January 2003, with harmonious echoes from former Canadian Ambassador to the United States Alan Gotlieb, Howe Institute author Wendy Dobson and others. Fearing a commercial backlash from the United States following Canada's refusal to endorse the U.S. war on Iraq, the

CCCE led nearly 100 chief executives to Washington in April 2003, meeting with business counterparts, politicians and diplomats, including Homeland Security Secretary Tom Ridge and While House Chief of Staff Andrew Card.

While deep integrationists have argued for trying to bring top U.S. policy makers on board the "big idea" train, there are Canadian business advocates arguing for a more incremental approach. Anne Golden, the chair of the Conference Board, suggests that the "concept of a grand tradeoff is flawed" and that the "devil is in the details" when you try to link economic policy and security preoccupations. Linkage itself is questionable. Like many Canadian critics of the "big idea", she cites experience in previous attempts to remove the threat of the use of U.S. trade remedy laws, as in the bilateral CUFTA. Golden argues for a pragmatic and timely series of incremental initiatives, building on the "smart border" program and moving toward a customs union.[106] But even an incremental approach raises doubts among careful observers. As Andrew Jackson of the Canadian Labour Congress concludes, in agreement with political scientist Stephen Clarkson, "the 'big idea'…conceals a lot of smaller ideas that are potential time-bombs."[107]

Among the most pungent time-bombs in the Conference Board approach is the proposal for a customs union. Even strong advocates of the original FTAs argue against it. Canadian free-trade "guru" Richard Lipsey, states:

> As a superpower, the United States would dominate any "joint" decision on common commercial policy…If Canadian policy were to change and try and push NAFTA into a full customs union, or even accept passively that this was to happen, it would entail a severe loss of Canadian independence in the sphere of foreign policy. We would have to dance to the Americans' tune on what they call trade policy, but which is really political foreign policy.[108]

An incremental approach characterizes perhaps the most important official Canadian document to treat the issues of North American relations in recent years, the voluminous December 2002 report, *Partners in North America,* by the parliamentary Standing Committee on Foreign Affairs and International Trade. The report proposes that North America be the subject of a coherent public strategy, with a strong, credible strategic framework that it addresses in 39 recommendations, capped with a proposal for formal North American leaders' summits that are supported by a permanent secretariat or commission and a permanent NAFTA court on trade and investment. As distinct from many of the business and policy think-tank approaches, the Standing Committee's report includes Mexico as a constituent element in its approach rather than as an afterthought.[109]

If one accepts that there is hardly a domestic policy issue in Canada that will not be fundamentally shaped by Canada's place in North America, the issue of the inadequacy of structures of democratic participation and accountability at the North American level emerges directly and urgently. The pressure for greater integration and the predominance of market values and efficiencies is considerable and comes from elites who may or may not embody the same priorities as their publics. For example, the upper echelons of the private sector are markedly more positive about integration and Americanization than are either the general public or the public-sector elite.

## IV. Intervention, War and the Bush Doctrine

The exercise of U.S. military, economic and diplomatic power in pursuit of a newly aggressive and interventionist foreign and security policy doctrine has placed greatly increased strain on bilateral and trilateral relations. The exercise of the unilateral "right" to undertake pre-emptive and so-called preventative aggressions against alleged threats to U.S. security has further undermined multilateral processes and institutions, which were already suffering from the Bush administration's rejection of the International Criminal Court and the Kyoto accord, among others.

U.S. "exceptionalism" conflicts in a variety of ways with the Canadian posture of support for multilateral diplomacy and peace-keeping. Stephanie Golub of CUNY characterizes the U.S. stance as essentially an inward-orientation, dominated by concern over a failing economy and security. Canada, on the other hand, is essentially outward-oriented, considerably pre-occupied with the United States, and thus vulnerable, particularly when it seems to be a "partnership with a society that expects its limited state to focus exclusively on its own internal problems and sees the international context as something to act upon, rather than act within."[110]

The Bush Administration's aggressive posture in the Middle East and with Iraq has excited considerable negative response among the Canadian populace, despite the extensive "spillover" of U.S. media and continued economic dependence. This, in turn, has placed the government under a great deal of strain, splitting its parliamentary caucus and resulting in considerable ambiguity of expression, but finally leading to a decision not to participate in the U.S./U.K. war on Iraq on the key grounds that it was not authorized by the UN Security Council, and further, that "regime change" by such unilateral military action was an extremely dangerous precedent. This posture, while popular with the public, and coincident to a large extent with the position taken by NAFTA-partner Mexico, marked a significant change from Canada's participation in the 1991 Gulf War. The government, however, increased the ambiguity of its stance by reinforcing Canadian naval cooperation in "anti-terrorist" activities in the Persian Gulf and sending a fresh contingent to assist international military presence in Afghanistan.

Canadian business and right-wing opposition leaders, together with the largest press and media conglomerate in the country, have been vociferous in their criticism of the government's position. As one of the more level-headed national columnists typified the 2002-2003 march to war, "When the Bush administration settled on war with Iraq, as it did many months ago, this media chorus began pounding the drums for Canada to get with the program, 'support our friends', 'liberate Iraq'. If not, Canada would be consigned to a 'marginal presence' in the world, which meant Washington, and would suffer terrible economic consequences."[111]

As noted above, the debate over the war led Canadian business leaders to reinforce their calls for deep integration, laced with pledges of friendship and a mass visit to Washington. The business press carried a number of stories filled with apprehension regarding U.S. economic retaliation, and the U.S. Ambassador added gasoline to the flames of fear, expressing the Bush Administration's "disappointment" with Canada. More particularly, Canadian businesses seeking contracts and sub-contracts for projects that are part of the multi-billion dollar rebuilding of Iraq feared being left in the cold.[112] On the other hand, Richard Perle, one of the leading U.S. war ideologues and businessmen, assayed that the two economies were so far integrated "that a backlash against one is a backlash against the other."[113]

Stephanie Golub notes that, despite the trade agreements and the American "orbit" they represent, "Canadian foreign policy continued to carve out a distinct image and role for Canada abroad as a champion of rule-based governance, against contrasting American unilateralism and asserting Canada's substantive ties to issues such a development and peace (especially seen in the government's support for the campaign to ban land mines)."[114] It appears the integrationist business elite is quite willing to cede this autonomy and initiative in favor of commercial reassurance.

# V. Convergence and/or Divergence: Future in Question

Canada will have a new government, albeit of the same party, within a year. The designated successor to Prime Minister Chrétien, Paul Martin, is closely identified with the business elite and has close U.S. ties. The current official opposition Canadian Alliance party, which has an almost knee-jerk affection for U.S. initiatives, has been losing public support, while the smaller social-democratic New Democratic Party saw its poll support double with the election of a new leader and a clear anti-war posture.

These developments could augur for extended public debate about the North American relationship. President Bush and his colleagues are currently a polarizing factor in Canada as elsewhere. The attempt of the Canadian business elite to garner a "strategic deal" with the Administration faces an unfriendly context.

Support for the project of deep integration drops off sharply when you leave elite conference rooms and the editorial pages of the corporate press. The project is essentially an elite one. A poll released in August 2002 indicates that Canadians "of all political stripes are uncomfortable with the level of influence the United States has over Canada's affairs." Almost 75 percent react to elite influence, indicating that the wealthy have too much influence on government.

While general Canadian amiability about the American people continues, and support for mutually beneficial economic cooperation is a strong as ever, Canadian expression of values and goals are more and more divergent from market-dominated U.S. society. Canadian political elites are more liberal than their U.S. counterparts. Canadians place a healthy population and clean environment second and third in policy priority, while for U.S. citizens they are seventh and eight, respectively. These divergences are expressed in graphic terms whether the issue is patriarchy in the family or gun control.[115]

A further obstacle is the inward posture of U.S. elites. "What is most striking about the new debate on North America in Canada is the eerie silence it is meeting on the U.S. side of the border, both in and out of government," notes Golub. "Despite statements to the contrary by Bush's proactive ambassador in Ottawa, interest in negotiating with the Canadians is a low-priority issue in a Washington [preoccupied with] an invasion of Iraq."[116]

Despite this apparent lack of an enthusiastic dancing partner, the actual or assumed political pressure from Washington, combined with the extensive investment in economic integration celebrated in NAFTA, puts a chill on Canadian foreign policy. Speaking to the CCCE in Washington in April 2003, former U.S. ambassador to Canada Tom Niles warned that there could be further difficulties in the post-war period if, for example, "Canada decides it will only participate in a reconstruction effort led by the UN." If Canada insists on a multilateral approach through the UN, "there might well be a problem. Because clearly that's not what is going to happen."[117] Once again, multilateralist preferences confront U.S. unilateralism and power. "My way or the highway." (Chrétien has declared that Canada will help pay for reconstruction whether it is directed by the United States or by the United Nations.)

The constraints are much deeper and more long-term, however. University of Toronto Professor Stephen Clarkson, who has written extensively on Canada/U.S. relations, looks at the broader overall framework of NAFTA. He declares that NAFTA is essentially a "supra-Constitution". It empowers some important actors and dis-empowers civil-society organizations and those citizens who look to the state to resolve problems. Those who enjoy and exploit their rights under NAFTA (and the WTO) are corporations.

Further integration based on the current model will only worsen things. It "increases the power asymmetries between the Canadian and American governments while reducing the power of the Canadian state vis-à-vis market forces," with further negative impacts on civil society and the ordinary citizen. From the economic dynamic emerges a profound political and democratic question.[118]

NAFTA as currently experienced contains within itself a central conundrum which was neatly summarized in the report of a study tour undertaken by a group of Canadian officials and researchers to the U.S.-Mexico border area in May 2002. They cited the need in a "NAFTA-Plus" accord to go beyond the "silent integration" of markets and deal with the social dimensions that are a by-product of economic development. Such a new agreement, with policies on environment, labor, energy, services, transport and other elements, would "need to go beyond NAFTA's current reach and implement governance structures by which these would be governed."[119] But this sort of prospect, something akin to the European model, finds little currency among the integrationist business elite, and probably even less among the members of the U.S. Congress or the Mexican or Canadian Parliaments.

An alternate model based on the assurance of greater "policy space" and renewed democracy in each country may be emerging. The politics of achieving it are as yet underdeveloped.

# Chapter 5
# Investment Provisions Threaten Democracy in All Three Countries
by Karen Hansen-Kuhn[120], Sarah Anderson[121], and John Foster

No single provision in NAFTA has generated more controversy in all three countries than the "investor-state" clause, which gives foreign investors the right to sue governments for compensation over public-interest laws that might undermine their profits. It presents a serious threat to local, regional and national governments' ability to establish rules to serve the public good.

The "investor-state" provision was an innovation in NAFTA. While it had been included in certain bilateral investment treaties and country-specific mixed claims commissions, NAFTA was the first trade agreement to incorporate such a mechanism. Previous trade agreements had included government-to-government processes designed to resolve issues related to expropriation of property, such as when a government takes possession of land in order to build a road. NAFTA's investor-state provision, however, dramatically expanded that practice, allowing companies to bypass local governments and court systems and to sue over "indirect" expropriation, meaning that virtually any governmental measure that might diminish their profits is subject to complaint and compensation. This kind of provision was also included in the proposed Multilateral Agreement on Investment and was a key factor in its rejection by France and other developed countries.

Corporations seeking damages under the investor-state clause take their claims to special NAFTA tribunals assembled under the auspices of the United Nations Commission for International Trade and Law (UNCITRAL) and the International

Center for Settlement of Disputes (ICSID) at the World Bank. Unless the parties agree otherwise, the hearings are held entirely in secret, with no obligation to release a written record, allow any type of participation of private citizens, NGOs, or state or local government officials, or even reveal details of the rulings. For most of the cases to date, the tribunals have been held in secret and participation restricted. Tribunals supercede the authority of national and state courts and there is no appellate body to ensure that mistakes in legal interpretation are corrected.

The investor-state clause has been a lightening rod for public debate on NAFTA, with critics raising concerns about the fact that it provides foreign investors greater rights than domestic investors, that it threatens democratically enacted public-interest laws, and that the decisionmaking process is so secretive. At a meeting of the NAFTA Commission on 31 July 2001, the Canadian, U.S. and Mexican trade ministers issued a "clarification" of the investor-state provision, as provided for under Article 1131 of NAFTA. The Commission pledged to increase the transparency of the process, making available all documents submitted to, or issued by, the investor-state tribunals, except in limited circumstances, and to share all relevant documents with their respective federal, state and provincial officials. Critics quickly responded that lacking an actual amendment of NAFTA, international arbitration rules would prevail and that "the regime of secrecy provided by the arbitral rules is both explicit and clear." In fact, prior to the clarification, the U.S. NGO Public Citizen had filed a Freedom of Information Act lawsuit to obtain information on the UPS vs. Canada case. Despite the governments' supposed commitment to transparency, they did not did not release the documents related to that case, and Public Citizen was forced to continue with its lawsuit.

Corporations also appear to be taking steps to ensure secrecy in the process since the "clarification" was issued. Investor-state cases can be adjudicated by panels operating under ICSID or UNCITRAL rules. While neither body provides adequate mechanisms for transparency, ICSID does publish some information on pending cases pending and their resolution on its website. No documents on cases brought before UNCITRAL are readily available. Only one case brought since that "clarification" has been tried in ICSID; the remainder either call for arbitration under UNCITRAL or do not indicate where the cases should be tried. Third parties, including the Council of Canadians and the Center for International Environmental Law have sought to participate in the cases, so far without any positive results.

There is also evidence that companies are using the treat of investor-state cases to discourage governments from even considering the passage of new public-interest laws. Lobbyists for the U.S. tobacco giants Phillip Morris and RJ Reynolds threatened such a suit when the Canadian government considered requiring plain packaging for cigarettes. The government quietly withdrew the measure. Journalist William Greider reported in *The Nation* that a former Canadian government official told him, "I've seen the letters from the New York and DC law firms coming up to the Canadian government on virtually every new environmental regulation and proposition in the last five years. They involved dry-cleaning chemicals, pharmaceuticals, pesticides, patent law. Virtually all of the new initiatives were targeted and most of them never saw the light of day."[122]

Twenty-seven cases have been filed under this provision to date (see Table 5-1), with the number of cases nearly evenly divided among the three countries. Eight cases involve challenges to national or local environmental regulations. The most-well known case in Mexico was brought by the U.S. based Metalclad Corporation, which was granted $15.6 million in damages over a municipal government's refusal to grant it a permit to operate a toxic-waste dump. The waste site, which had not been properly maintained, was leaching toxic residues

## Table 5-1
## NAFTA Investor-State Cases to Date

| Case | Venue | Damages Sought (US$) | Status | Issue |
|------|-------|------|--------|-------|
| Ethyl v. Canada Sept. 1996 | UNCITRAL | $201 million | Settled; $13 million paid to Ethyl | U.S. chemical company challenges environmental regulation of gasoline additive MMT |
| Metalclad v. Mexico Jan. 1997 | ICSID | $90 million | Metalclad wins $15.6 million | U.S. firm challenges Mexican municipality's refusal to grant construction permit for toxic waste dump. |
| Azinian v. Mexico Mar. 1997 | ICSID | $19 million | Dismissed | U.S. companies challenge Mexican court's revocation of waste management contract for suburb of Mexico City |
| Waste Management v. Mexico Oct. 1998 | ICSID | $60 million | Dismissed on jurisdiction; resubmitted. Decision pending. | U.S. company challenges City of Acapulco revocation of waste disposal concession |
| Loewen v. USA Oct. 1998 | ICSID | $725 million | Pending | Canadian funeral company challenges Mississippi jury damage award |
| S.D. Myers v. Canada Oct. 1998 | UNCITRAL | $20 million | S.D. Myers wins | U.S. waste treatment company challenges Canadian ban of PCB exports in compliance with multilateral environmental agreement |
| Sun Belt v. Canada Nov. 1998 | UNCITRAL | $10.5 million | Pending. Appears to not to have progressed to arbitration. | U.S. water company challenges British Columbia's moratorium on bulk water exports |
| Pope & Talbot v. Canada Dec. 1998 | UNCITRAL | $381 million | Pope & Talbot wins $461,566 | U.S. timber company challenges Canada's implementation of 1996 U.S.-Canada Softwood Lumber Agreement |
| Feldman v. Mexico Apr. 1999 | ICSID | $50 million | Karpa loses on issue of expropriation, wins on national treatment | U.S. cigarette exporter challenges denial of export tax rebate by Mexican govt. |
| Methanex v. USA Jul. 1999 | UNCITRAL | $970 million | Dismissed, resubmitted on more limited grounds | Canadian company challenges California phase-out of gasoline additive MTBE |
| Mondev v. USA Sept. 1999 | ICSID | $50 million | Dismissed | Canadian real estate developer challenges Massachussetts Supreme Court ruling on local government sovereign immunity. |
| UPS v. Canada Jan. 2000 | UNCITRAL | $160 million | Pending | U.S. company claims Canadian post office unfairly subsidizes local parcel delivery service |
| Adams v. México Jan. 2000 | UNCITRAL | $75 million | Pending | U.S. landowner challenges Mexican court ruling on real estate title |
| ADF Group v. USA Jul. 2000 | ICSID | $90 million | Dismissed | Canadian steel contractor challenges U.S. "Buy America" law |
| Ketcham v. Canada Dec. 2000 | | $19.5 million | Withdrawn | U.S. company challenges Canadian implementation of 1996 U.S.-Canada Softwood Lumber Agreement |

| | | | | |
|---|---|---|---|---|
| Trammell Crow v. Canada Jul. 2001 | UNCITRAL | $32 million | Settled | U.S. real estate developer challenges Canada Post outsourcing of real estate management service. |
| Crompton v. Canada Nov. 2001 | | $100 million | Pending | U.S. company challenges Canadian ban on use of lindane in fertilizer |
| Canfor v. USA Nov. 2001 | UNCITRAL | $250 million | Pending | Canadian timber company challenges US countervailing duties on softwood lumber |
| Fireman's Fund v. Mexico Nov. 2001 | ICSID | $50 million | Pending | U.S. company challenges Mexican government's discrimination against dollar-denominated over peso-denominated debentures |
| Calmark v. México Jan. 2002 | | $400,000 | Pending | U.S. company challenges Mexican court's handling of legal dispute on cancelled land sale |
| Kenex v. USA Jan. 2002 | UNCITRAL | $20 million | Pending | Canadian company challenges U.S. confiscation of industrial hemp seeds |
| Frank v. Mexico Feb. 2002 | UNCITRAL | $1.5 million | Pending | U.S. investor challenges Mexican court's handling of dispute over development of beachfront property |
| Baird v. USA March 2002 | | $13 billion | Pending | Canadian investor challenges U.S. rules on disposal of nuclear waste. |
| Gami v. Mexico Apr. 2002 | UNCITRAL | $27 million | Pending | U.S. investor challenges changes to Mexican subsidies to and regulation of sugar industry |
| Doman v. USA May 2002 | | $513 million | Pending | Canadian company challenges U.S. countervailing duties on softwood lumber |
| Tembec v. USA May 2002 | | $200 million | Pending | Canadian company challenges U.S. countervailing duties on softwood lumber |
| Thunderbird v. México March 2002 | UNCITRAL | $100 million | Pending | U.S. investor challenges Mexican government's regulation and closure of its gambling facilities |

Sources: www.naftalaw.org; Canadian Foreign Affairs website (http://www.dfait-maeci.gc.ca/tna-nac/NAFTA-en.asp) ; U.S. Department of State website http://www.state.gov/s/l/c3439.htm; Public Citizen, NAFTA Chapter 11 Investor-to-State Cases: Bankrupting Democracy, 24 September 2001; *Canada Newswire*, "Softwood Lumber: Tembec announces its intention to file a claim against the U.S. under NAFTA", 5 May 2002.
Canadian Methanex Corporation is demanding $970 million in compensation for a California ban of MTBE, a chemical that can cause cancer and was leaching into local

into the local water supply. When Metalclad purchased the dump, the local government required that the company clean up the site and provide safeguards before reopening it for business. Metalclad successfully argued that this constituted an indirect expropriation of its business under the NAFTA investor-state rules.

Both the Canadian and U.S. governments have been sued over bans on hazardous gasoline additives. The U.S.-based Ethyl Corporation brought a case against the Canadian government for its ban of MMT, a nerve toxin. The Canadian government settled the case by ending the ban and paying Ethyl $13 million in compensation. The groundwater. In each of these cases, the public danger presented by the banned chemicals or unsafe waste dump was not at issue, only the loss of actual or potential profits, which in most cases went well beyond any funds actually invested in the projects.

The Feldman Karpa vs. Mexico case also produced alarming results. Feldman, a cigarette exporter, won its case against Mexico alleging that it did not receive the same treatment as Mexican cigarette exporters – an illegal kickback on cigarette taxes. In his dissenting opinion on the case, arbitrator Jorge Covarrubias Bravo stated, "Thus, CEMSA's [Feldman's company] export business, being a legal activity, was based on premises that clearly violated Mexican laws: to obtain tax rebates from the government without being entitled to them."[123]

While some cases have been based on allegations that local court systems have not afforded foreign companies due process, most involve direct challenges to public policies. The U.S. based United Parcel Service claims that the Canada Post uses its monopoly on letter delivery to subsidize its courier service. This case also represents an attempt to expand the scope of investor-state challenges to competition policy, even though compensation for cases involving government monopolies was excluded from NAFTA's chapter on that issue. The Canadian Union of Postal Workers and the Council of Canadians have cited this case in a legal challenge to the constitutionality of the investor-state mechanism. CUPW President Deborah Bourque commented, "The UPS case shows how foreign corporations are using NAFTA to attack public services."[124]

The U.S. Pope and Talbot company recently won a case challenging Canada's implementation of the U.S.-Canada Softwood Lumber Agreement. Four Canadian firms have separately brought cases against the United States for its decisions on softwood lumber. Pierre Pettigrew, Canada's Minister for International Trade, describes the softwood lumber issue as the world's largest trade dispute, involving years of negotiations between the two governments. These companies have decided to bypass those government-to-government deliberations, seeking instead to force decisions at unaccountable arbitration boards.

There has been a heated public debate in all three countries on the investor-state mechanism. It became a major issue during discussions of Trade Promotion Authority in the U.S. Congress. Nevertheless, more and more cases are being raised on an ever-increasing array of issues. Although concern about this mechanism has become acute in a variety of quarters, there are significant corporate interests who want to extend the privileges it provides. In a joint letter from 29 multinationals to US Trade Representative Robert B. Zoellick in April 2001, corporate leaders sought expansion of the definition of expropriation to cover any government action or regulation that might 'diminish the value of investor's assets'.

None of the three governments has attempted to significantly change the investor-state provision in NAFTA and, in fact, efforts continue to extend it to other countries in the Americas. Despite instructions to USTR listed in the new Trade Promotion Authority that require changes in investor-state clauses in future trade agreements, the recently completed U.S.-Chile free-trade agreement continues to prohibit "indirect" expropriation and measures "tantamount" to expropriation with only minor modifications from the NAFTA model.[125] Mexico has signed numerous trade agreements with other Latin American and Caribbean countries, all of which contain investor-state language very similar to that in NAFTA. And despite it pledges to oppose the mechanism in the FTAA, the Canadian government has yet take actions to promote major changes in that clause within the draft accord. Instead, the three governments should listen to the chorus of disapproval emerging from civil-society, as well as state and local legislatures, and move to eliminate this undemocratic and unfair provision from NAFTA and any other future accord.

# Endnotes

1   Alternatives for the Americas, produced a collective effort by members of the Hemispheric Social Alliance (HSA). The fourth version is available at www.asc-hsa.org in Spanish and English. The translation to German is underway. The second version was published in five languages: English; Spanish; French; Portuguese; and Creole.

2   Researcher at the Universidad Autónoma Metropolitana (UAM) and member of the Mexican Action Network on Free Trade (RMALC) coordination team and the Operating Committee of the Hemispheric Social Alliance.

3   The author of this essay has published much broader and more detailed analyses of the issues covered here. The broadest of these, although based on information on just the first five years of NAFTA can be found in Arroyo, Alberto (coordinator), El TLCAN 5 años depués, Contenido, Resultados y Propuestas. Published in CD. Comisión de Comercio H Cámara de Diputados LVII Legislatura 2000 (415 pages). A less detailed but more recent análisis can be found in the book: Arroyo, Alberto, Resultados del Tratado de Libre Comercio de América del Norte en México: Lecciones para las Negociaciones del Area de Libre Comercio de las Américas, Ediciones RMALC, México, March 2002.

4   Grupo de Trabajo Instituto Nacional de Geografía e Informática (INEGI), Secretaría de Hacienda (SHCP) and Banco de México (BM) taken from INEGI electronic databases (BIE/INEGI). Additional referentes in parentheses in this paper refer to the methods used to access the data in electronic databases or web pages. All information refers to the NAFTA period, up to December 2002.

5   INEGI, SHCP and BM, taken from www.shcp.gob.mx/info/html/mex08.html.

6   INEGI, SHCP and BM, taken from BIE-INEGI (foreign sector/trade balance by geographic zones and countries).

7   INEGI, SHCP and BM. Taken from BIE-INEGI (foreign sector/summary of foreign trade/current presentation/exports/total).

8   INEGI, SCCP and BM. Taken from BIE-INEGI (foreign sector/Mexican balance of payments/current account balance).

9   Taken from BIE-INEGI (energy sector/monthly indicators/petroleum subsector/exports/crude petroleum/by region/Americas). There

is a small inflation of the data since they deal with exports to the Americas as a whole and not just to the United States, but in fact the vast majority is to that country.

10 Calculations based on data from INEGI, SHCP and BM trade balance. Taken from www.shcp.gob.mx.

11 *Expansión* magazine.

12 INEGI, SHCP, and BM. Taken from BIE-INEGI (foreign sector-trade balance by geographic zone and country/exports/United States/ imports/United States). Does not include Puerto Rico or Virgin Islands. Includes maquiladora exports.

13 INEGI Estadísticas Industria Maquiladora de Exportación. Taken from BIE-INEGI (Maquiladora Export Industry/Monthly Indicators/by Federal Entity/National Total/National Inputs)

14 Calculation by Héctor Vázquez Tercero, "Medición del flujo efectivo de divisas en la balanza comercial de México," in *Comercio Exterior*, Ed. Banco de Comercio Exterior August 1995, Table 5, p. 599. The 1995 and 1996 data were provided to the autor courtesy of Vázquez Tercero.

15 Ibid.

16 Secretaría de Economía. Comisión Nacional de Inversiones Extranjeras. "Informe estadístico sobre el comportamiento de la inversión extranjera directa en México" Table 2 by economic sector. Taken from www.economia.gob.mx.

17 Calculations based on *Expansión* magazine.

18 See SECOFI, the Ministry of Trade and Industrial Development, now the Ministry of the Economy, *Tratado de Libre Comercio de América del Norte* Ed. Porrua 1993. Chapter IV articles 401 to 403 and the analysis carried out by Andrés Peñalosa in *El Tratado de Libre Comercio de América del Norte. Análisis Critica y Propuesta* P. 79-88

19 Interview by the author with the owner, Ing. Rubén Barrios Graff.1997. On conditions agreed to in the FTAs, see Jorge Calderón and Alberto Arroyo (coordinators) *El Tratado de libre Comercio de América del Norte -Análisis Crítica y Propuesta* Edited by the Red Mexicana de Acción frente al Libre Comercio (RMALC) México 1993.and Andrés Peñalosa and Alberto Arroyo (coordinators) *Acuerdo de Asociación Económica, Concertación Política y Cooperación entre México y la Unión Europea.* Red Mexicana de Acción Frente al Libre Comercio. México 2000

20 See especially *Tratado de Libre Comercio de América del Norte* op. cit. chapters XV, X, XI y III: Also the corresponding analysis in Alberto Arroyo and Jorge Calderón (coordinators) *El Tratado de Libre Comercio de América del Norte. Análisis Crítica y Propuesta* op. cit

21 Source: Banco de México, Balance of Payments. Taken from BIE-INEGI (Foreign sector/Mexican balance of payments/capital account/liabilities/foreign investment).

22 Secretaría de la Economía. Comisión Nacional de Inversiones Extranjeras. "Informe estadística sobre el comportamiento de la inversión extranjera directa en México" Table 1. Taken from www.economia.gob.mx.

23 Ibid Table 2 by economic sector.

24 Ibid. Table 5. By federal registry entity.

25 The statistical information does not allow for the separation of what is purchases of companies from new investments. However, it is enough that each year one adds the value of the main companies that have been sold and compare them with the total amount. For example, in 2001 the sale of Banamex is half of the direct foreign investment for that year.

26 All data on foreign portfolio investment (stock and bonds) are from the Banco de México. Taken from BIE-INEGI (financial sector/ Mexican balance of payments/capital account/liabilities/foreign investment).

27 An analysis of the 1994 Mexican peso crisis can be found in Alberto Arroyo, "La Crisis Mexicano y el modelo de desarrollo," in *Tenemos Propuesta*, edited by the Red Mexicana de Acción frente al Libre Comercio, September 1995, p. 3-15.

28 See SECOFI, *Tratado de Libre Comercio de América del Norte*. Ed. Purrua México 1993. Chapter 11 and critical análisis in Arroyo and Calderón *Tratado de Libre Comercio de América del Norte. Análisis, Crítica y Propuesta*. Ed. RMALC México 1993. Chapter 11.

29 This issue and the investor-state cases are detailed in a separate essay in this publication.

30 Calculation based on GDP data from INEGI *Sistema de Cuentas Nacionales* and average rate of population growth from *Censos Generales de Población y Vivienda*.

31 Calculation by Dr. Alejandro Villamar based on data from INEGI *Sistema Nacional de Cuentas Económicas y Ecológicas de México*, 1988-1996 various tables, and 1993-1999, Table 2.

32   INEGI National Employment Surveys 1993 to 2003 1993 table 57; 1995, table 70; 1997-1999, table 3.38; 2000, table 3.46; 2001-2002, table 3.39. First quarter of 2003. Strategic indicators of employment and unemployment.

33   INEGI National Employment Surveys 1993-2003. 1993, table 66; 1995, table 73; 1996-1999, table 3.39; 2000 table 3.65; 2001-2002 table 3.39; First quarter of 2003. Strategic indicators of employment and unemployment.

34   INEGI National Employment Surveys 1993-2003. 1993, table 72; 1995, table 167; 1996-2002, table 3.73; First quarter of 2003. Strategic indicators of employment and unemployment.

35   IMSS Monthly Report on the Population. Taken from www.stps.gov.mx.

36   Calculation based on INEGI, Banco de México and SHCP, taken from www.shcp.gob.mx/html/mex08.html.

37   Secretaría de la Economía, "Informe estadístico sobre el comportamiento de la inversión extranjera en México", Table 2. Taken from www.economia.gob.mx.

38   INEGI. Manufacturing GDP. Nacional accounting system. Productivity. Employment. Monthly industrial surveys taken from BIE-INEGI and www.inegi.gob.mx.

39   INEGI Monthly Industrial Survey and Banco de México Economic Indicators. Taken from www.inegi.gob.mx. Indicators of competitiveness of the manufacturing sector.

40   INEGI Maquiladora Export Industry Statistics. Taken from BIE-INEGI (maquiladora export industry/annual indicators/by federal entity/national total/productivity index). 1993=100%.

41   INEGI Mquiladora Export Industry Statistics. Taken from BIE-INEGI (Maquiladora export industry/annual indicators/by state/national total/employed persons)

42   PIAI-CIESTAAM Coordinator. Phone/Fax: 0052(595)952-1506. Email: ciestaam@avantel.net

43   CIESTAAM Director, Member of the PIAI Technical Committee. Phone/Fax: 0052(595)952-1613. Email: rsr@avantel.net

44   CIESTAAM, 1992, La agricultura mexicana frente al Tratado Trilateral de Libre Comercio. Mexico City: Juan Pablos, p. 10.

45   World Bank, Memorandum from the President of the *Banco Internacional de Reconstrucción y Fomento* and the *Corporación Financiera Internacional* to the Executive Directorate, on "Estrategia de Asistencia para el País del Grupo del Banco Mundial para los

Estados Unidos Mexicanos. Unidad para Colombia–México–Venezuela." Report No. 23849-ME, April 23, 2002, pp. 12-13, http://bancomundial.org.mx/- pdf/EAP_Documento_Principal.pdf.

[46] In early 2003, the Mexican government reduced, for example, the prices of electricity and diesel fuel used in agriculture, although numerous bureaucratic hurdles are involved.

[47] The Mexican government established safeguard measures for the nation's poultry industry, which is the most technologically advanced, and furthermore, the industry that is most integrated with the United States, due to the capital originating from that country.

[48] USDA, *Farm Bill 2002*, Information Homepage, http://www.usda.gov/farmbill/index.html

[49] OECD, 2002, *Agricultural Compendium*, Producer and Consumer Support Estimates 2002, data base, Beyond 20/20 Browser Files. Paris, France, *op. cit.*

[50] Authors' calculation based on information from OECD, 2002.

[51] It is worth clarifying here that the OECD methodology illustrates the distortion caused by the exchange rate in the case of Mexico. Since Mexico has a notoriously over-valued exchange rate, agricultural assistance is over-estimated. If we use a balanced exchange rate, the subsidy increases to 14% in 2001 in Mexico, or in other words, it represents 39% of the assistance provided in the US.

[52] 1 hectare (ha) = 2.47109 acres.

[53] Authors' calculations based on: SECOFI, 1994. *Tratado de Libre Comercio de América del Norte. Fracciones arancelarias y plazos de desgravación, México.* Miguel Ángel Porrúa Book Publisher and USDA, ERS, Foreign Agricultural Trade of the United States, http://www.fas.usda.gov/ustrdscripts/ USReport.exe)

[54] INEGI, *Banco de Información Económica* (BIE), External Sector, Importing of commodities by product and by economic activity of origin, http://www.inegi.gob.mx/difusion/espanol/fbie.html. 4.12.2002.

[55] Mexican President's Office, 2002, *Segundo Informe de Gobierno*, September 1, Annex, p. 237.

[56] Vollrath, Thomas L. and Paul V. Johnston. 'The Changing Structure of Agricultural Trade In North America, Pre and Post CUSTA/NAFTA: What Does It Mean?" AAEA/CAEA poster paper, (annual meetings), Chicago, August 5-8, 2001. http://www.ers.usda.gov/briefing/nafta/PDFFiles/Vollrath- 2001AAEAPoster.pdf

57    Department of Labor and Social Security (*Secretaría del Trabajo y Previsión Social*—STPS). National Employment Survey. Employed population, by sex and by branch of economic activity. http://www.stps.gob.mx/01_oficina/05_cgpeet/302_0055a.htm, 9.11.2002.

58    Fernando Cortés Cáceres, et al., 2002, Evolución y características de la pobreza en México en la última década del siglo XXI, Sedesol, August, p. 19.

59    Agroindustrialists producing beer and tequila; producers and packers of export vegetables and tropical fruits; importers of meat, grains, fruit and inputs.

60    *El Financiero*, 4.11.2002, p.26.

61    Information from Efrén Marín López, 2002, "La solución política: ¿Opción a la insuficiencia de los capítulos 19 y 20 del TLCAN?" doctoral dissertation, UAM, Xochimilco, Mexico City, December, pp. 90-102.

62    Public Citizen maintains a database of certified job losses under this program. See also see the US Department of Labor database www.doleta.gov/tradeact/taa/ntaa/asp/nafta.asp

63    Kate Bronfenbrenner, "Final Report: The Effects of Plant Closing or Threat of Plant Closing on Workers Right to Organize," Report to The Labor Secretariat of the North American Commission for Labor Cooperation, September 29, 1996. Kate Bronfenbrenner, "Uneasy Terrain: The Impact of Capital Mobility on Workers, Wages and Union Organizing," Report to the U.S. Trade Deficit Review Commission, September 6, 2000, www.ustdrc.gov. Also see, Robert E. Scott, "NAFTA's Hidden Costs," Economic Policy Institute Briefing Paper, April 2001, www.epinet.org/briefingpapers/nafta01.

64    Robert E. Scott, "NAFTA's Hidden Costs, April, 2001, www.epinet.org/briefingpapers/nafta01

65    U.S. Department of Labor, Bureau of Labor Statistics, Mass Layoff Statistics, www.data.bls.gov/cgi-bin/surveymost

66    Lawrence Mishel, Jared Bernstein and John Schmitt, *The State of Working America: 2000-2001*, Economic Policy Institute, Cornell University ILR Press: Ithaca, NY, 2001.

67    Heather Boushey, Chauna Brocht, Bethney Gundersen and Jared Bernstein, *Hardships In America: The Real Story of Working Families*, Washington D.C.: Economic Policy Institute, 2001

68    Calculations based on data from Mishell and Bernstein, *The State of Working America 2002-03*, Cornell University ILR Press, 2003.

[69] U.S. Department of Labor, Advisory Council on Employee Welfare and Pension Benefit Plans, *Report of the Working Group on the Benefit Implications of the Growth of a Contingent Workforce,* November 10, 1999, www.dol.gov/pwba/adcoun/contrpt

[70] Information based on Ken Hudson, "No Shortage of 'Nonstandard' Jobs," Economic Policy Institute Briefing Paper, December, 1999, www.epinet.org/briefingpapers/hudson and also Steven Hipple, "Contingent Work in the Late-1990s, *Monthly Labor Review,* March, 2001

[71] See in addition to above sources, Steven Hipple and Jay Stewart, "Earnings and Benefits of Contingent and Non-Contingent Workers," *Monthly Labor Review,* October 1996, pp. 22-30.

[72] William Grady, "Homeless not necessarily jobless," *Chicago Tribune,* December 19, 2002.

[73] Figures compiled by National Center for Policy Analysis, www.ncpa.org/pi/crime

[74] Data from U.S. Immigration and Naturalization Service, www.ins.usdoj.gov

[75] Emma Chavez, "Remittances and Development Policy in Mexico," Unpublished Master's Project, College of Urban Planning and Public Affairs, University of Illinois at Chicago, 2002.

[76] This problem is discussed by Jeff Faux, "Falling dollar, rising debt," *American Prospect,* July, 2002

[77] These figures come from the Federal Reserve Bank and were reported in the *Chicago Tribune,* December 15, 2002.

[78] Principal Researcher, North-South Institute, Ottawa, Canada.

[79] Researcher on global economic justice with KAIROS: Canadian Ecumenical Justice Initiatives.

[80] Jackson, Andrew, *From Leaps of Faith to Lapses of Logic: Assessing a Decade of Free Trade,* Ottawa: Canadian Labour Congress, 1999.

[81] Clarkson, Stephen, *Uncle Sam and Us, Globalization, Neoconservatism and the Canadian State,* Toronto, University of Toronto Press, 2002, p. 194.

[82] *Toronto Star,* 2 June 1999.

[83] Study by the Centre for the Study of Living Standards cited in *Globe and Mail,* 15 May 2001.

[84] *CCPA Monitor,* Vol. 9, No. 7, Dec 2002-Jan. 2003

[85] Hurtig, Mel (2002), *The Vanishing Country: Is It Too Late to Save Canada?* Toronto: McClelland and Stewart, pp. 52-53

[86] Ibid., p. 54.

87   *Inside US Trade*, 25 November 1988.

88   Campbell, Bruce; Gutierrez Haces, Maria Teresa; Jackson, Andrew; Larudee, Mehrene; Sanger, Matthew, *Pulling Apart: the Deterioration of Employment and income in North America under Free Trade*, Ottawa, Canadian Centre for Policy Alternatives, 1999, p. 100.

89   *Globe and Mail,* 11 January 2003.

90   Clarkson, p. 199.

91   Kerstetter, Steve, *Rags and Riches: Wealth Inequality in Canada,* Ottawa: Canadian Centre for Policy Alternatives, 2002.

92   Gutierrez-Haces, Teresa, "Smart Border and Security Perimeter in Canada", *Voices of Mexico*, Mexico City, 2002.

93   Golub, Stephanie R., *North America Beyond NAFTA? Sovereignty, Identity and Security in Canada-U.S. Relations*, Canadian-American Public Policy, Number 52, December 2002, Orono, Canadian-American Center, University of Maine.

94   Golden, Anne, "Building a new partnership", *The Globe and Mail*, Toronto, 5 March 2003 p. A11.

95   D'Aquino, Thomas, *Security and Prosperity: The Dynamics of a New Canada-United States Partnership in North America*, Presentation to the Annual General Meeting of the Canadian Council of Chief Executives, Toronto, January 14, 2003.

96   Clark, Campbell, "Canada, U.S. negotiating border deal, sources say," *The Globe and Mail*, Toronto, April 10, 2003 p. A22.

97   Golub, 2003.

98   House of Commons, Standing Committee on Foreign Affairs and International Trade (SCFAIT), *Partners in North America: Advancing Canada's Relations with the United States and Mexico*, Ottawa, House of Commons, 2002, p. 95-6.

99   SCFAIT, p. 102.

100   *Toronto Star,* 9 January 2003.

101   Dobson, Wendy, "The next big idea: Trade can brush in a new border," *The Globe and Mail*, Toronto, January 21, 2003. p. A15.

102   Dobbin, Murray, "Prescription for decline," *The Globe and Mail*, Toronto, 25 October 2002.

103   Seccareccia, Mario, *North American Monetary Integration: Should Canada Join the Dollarization Bandwagon?* Ottawa, Canadian Centre for Policy Alternatives, October, 2002, p.2.

104   Foster, 2002, p.10.

105   Foster, 2002.

106   Golden, 2003.

[107] Jackson, Andrew, *Why the "Big Idea" Is a Bad Idea,* Ottawa: Canadian Labour Congress, 2003, p. 4.

[108] Hurtig, p. 326-7.

[109] SCFAIT, 2002.

[110] Golub, p. 29.

[111] Simpson, Jeffrey, "Worried about U.S. retribution? Don't be," *The Globe and Mail,* Toronto, 9 April 2003.

[112] Brethour, Patrick, "Iraq a field of dreams for big oil firms," *The Globe and Mail,* Toronto, 10 April 2003 p. B1., and Varcoe, 2003, P. D1.

[113] Simpson, 2003.

[114] Golub, p. 12.

[115] Hurtig, part 4.

[116] Golub, p. 28.

[117] Stewart, Sinclair, "Warm U.S. welcome cheers CEOs," *Report on Business, The Globe and Mail,* Toronto, 8 April 2003, p.9.

[118] Clarkson, 2002.

[119] Public Policy Forum, The New Dynamics of North America: U.S.-Mexico Relations and the Border Economy, Ottawa, May, 2002.

[120] Co-ordinator of the Hemispheric Social Alliance Analysis Team, Latin American Analyst with The Development GAP and member of the Alliance for Responsible Trade

[121] Researcher at the Institute for Policy Studies and Member of the Alliance for Responsible Trade.

[122] Tobacco case and quote from Canadian official from William Greider, "The Right and US Trade Law: Invalidating the 20th Century", *The Nation,* 17 November 2001.

[123] Available at www.naftalaw.com.

[124] Cited in *Washington Trade Daily,* 2 June 2003.

[125] " The U.S.-Chile and U.S.-Singapore Free Trade Agreements: Report of the Labor Advisory Committee for Trade Negotiations and Trade Policy", 28 February 2003.